Words
You Should
Teach
Your
Children

Words
You Should
Teach
Your
Children

From *Character* and *Confidence*
to *Patience* and *Peace*

**200 ESSENTIAL WORDS FOR
RAISING YOUR CHILDREN**

PAULA BALZER

Aadamsmedia
Avon, Massachusetts

Published by
Adams Media, a division of F+W Media, Inc.
57 Littlefield Street, Avon, MA 02322. U.S.A.
www.adamsmedia.com

ISBN 10: 1-4405-5460-9
ISBN 13: 978-1-4405-5460-5
eISBN 10: 1-4405-5461-7
eISBN 13: 978-1-4405-5461-2

Printed in the United States of America.

10   9   8   7   6   5   4   3   2   1

This publication is designed to provide accurate and authoritative information with regard to the subject matter covered. It is sold with the understanding that the publisher is not engaged in rendering legal, accounting, or other professional advice. If legal advice or other expert assistance is required, the services of a competent professional person should be sought.

—From a *Declaration of Principles* jointly adopted by a Committee of the American Bar Association and a Committee of Publishers and Associations

Many of the designations used by manufacturers and sellers to distinguish their product are claimed as trademarks. Where those designations appear in this book and Adams Media was aware of a trademark claim, the designations have been printed with initial capital letters.

This book is available at quantity discounts for bulk purchases.
For information, please call 1-800-289-0963.

To Peter & June—for teaching me the real meaning of love, happiness, and fun.

Acknowledgments

One of the best things about writing a book is that you get the opportunity to publicly thank everyone who made it possible. Thank you to everyone at Adams Media, notably Ross Weisman, Brendan O'Neill, and Katie Corcoran Lytle. Thank you to my family (the Balzers, Vitales, and the Loderhose clan), and the friends who make my life as a parent easier, especially after moving to a new place: Jill Penman, Michele Bloom, Jess Parsons, David Halpern, Billy Kingsland, Stephen Serwin, Dena Koklanaris, Maya Baran, Nazie Furst, Heather Hamilton, Mame Hogan, and Jennifer and Jason Levesque. And of course, Peter and June.

Contents

Introduction

Do you want your children to treat others with *respect*, *humility*, and *gratitude*?

Do you want your children to have a good sense of *responsibility*, *integrity*, and *conviction*?

Do you want your children to have *confidence*, a good sense of *humor*, and a good amount of *motivation*?

Of course you do! You're a parent and you want your kids to grow up into kind, generous, well-rounded individuals who value your *family* and their friends and care for others. But how do you make sure you're raising strong, well-adjusted, loyal, happy children? You can start by talking to your kids about the things that are important to you and making sure that they understand the true meaning of words that adults use to express *love*, *fear*, *faith*, and other crucial ideas.

In *Words You Should Teach Your Children*, you'll find 200 words that will help you teach your kids about the important concepts that make us better people by clearly defining the words that they need to know. Each entry contains a pronunciation guide, the word's definition and part of speech, a sample sentence, and information on why that particular word is one that your children should understand and embody as they grow. Use these words when you chat with your kids and reinforce the ideas behind them in the ways that you show your affection to others, interact with your neighbors, and ultimately live your life. As a parent, you are your child's first and most important teacher and you have a lot of teaching to do. So enjoy it. Your children are only young once!

The
Words
You Should

Teach
Your
Children

achievement

(uh-CHEEV-ment)

noun

Success in a particular area after exerting great effort.

Finishing my school report on birds after weeks of work felt like a major ACHIEVEMENT.

When you think of the word "achievement," it's easy to think of major milestones: graduation, acceptance to college, or a first job. While these are important achievements, be sure to enjoy all the little ones along the way. Praise your child for learning to catch a baseball, learning the alphabet, or riding a bike for the first time. It's certainly easy to remember graduation day, but you won't remember the joy on your child's face as he hits his first baseball unless you specifically make a point to. These are treasured memories and you'll be glad to have them. If your child is able to understand and recognize that his achievements—big *and* small—are something to be proud of and strive for, he'll be more likely than ever to put extra effort into reaching his goals.

acknowledge

(ack-NOLL-idj)

verb

To show awareness or express thanks for someone's behavior.

I'm always sure to ACKNOWLEDGE my friends when they do something special for me.

Adults know how pleasant it is to be acknowledged. Whether someone comments on a job well done at work, or notices a new haircut—it's nice to know that others are aware of us. It's easy to acknowledge a child's accomplishments—like a good grade, a ballet recital—and it's also easy to acknowledge their bad behavior. Make it a point to positively acknowledge your child frequently. Comment on how you appreciate the way she remembers to say "good morning" or that you like the shirt she chose to wear. Your child will feel appreciated, and will soon learn to extend such courtesies to others.

admire

(ad-MY-er)

verb

To view another person or object with pleasure and approval.

I really ADMIRE my soccer coach—she's such a talented player.

Adults admire people for their intelligence, passion, and talent. You may find that your child admires someone completely different every day. One day it might be you, the next day a teacher or superhero. Talk to your children about the qualities you admire in other people. Show them that there are specific traits that make a person deserving of your praise. Talk about the value of intelligence, passion, kindness, and innovation. Your children will soon begin to understand what makes a person admirable, and will make good choices about whom they choose to admire.

adventure

(ad-VEN-chur)

noun

An unusual and sometimes daring experience.

I had never slept in the woods before, so camping with my family felt like a true ADVENTURE.

Children love a good adventure, and the good thing about planning an adventure for children is that you can plan anything that feels different from their regular routine. For example, eating a picnic dinner in your backyard will feel like an adventure to a young child. You can let your kids build a fort in the attic, or take them for a walk in the country. Teaching your children that an adventure of any kind is a positive experience—and not something to be feared—will boost their confidence as they venture into the world on their own.

angry

(ANG-gree)

adjective

Feeling mad, either at someone else or about a particular situation.

I can't help but feel ANGRY when things don't go my way at school.

Anger is unavoidable and can be brought on by anything—losing your keys, forgetting a file at the office, or being hurt by a family member or friend. Your child may be angry about not getting a part in the school play, being excluded in the lunch room, or about losing an important soccer game. You need to show your children that, while anger is normal, it's important to let go of the things that make us angry. Children feel anger quickly, both on the playground and at home when they don't get their way; luckily, children naturally get over their anger just as quickly. Be sure to help your children hold on to this quality by showing them how to move on and forgive when something makes them angry.

apology

(uh-POL-uh-jee)

noun

Words or actions that show you are sorry for something you said or did.

I owe my mother an APOLOGY for not being a good listener yesterday.

Saying you're sorry isn't easy for anyone—especially children. You can start teaching them to apologize by setting an example. We all have difficult moments as parents, and you should not hesitate to apologize for your behavior when necessary. It's also helpful to show children that a heartfelt apology can make a friend or family member feel much better. Children make mistakes, as we all do—they forget to share, don't always take turns—and feelings are easily hurt. Let them see how such actions can be remedied with a simple "I'm sorry."

appreciation

(uh-pree-shee-A-shun)

noun

An expression of thanks for the things you have or for the people in your life and how they make it better.

I have so much APPRECIATION for my loving parents, my pet, and even my brand new bicycle.

Life can be challenging, which may make it easy for your children to forget that there's much to appreciate. Think about what you truly value—your family, your home, your friends—and take the time to be grateful and let people know that you appreciate them being part of your world. While most children have much to be grateful for, it's okay to let them know that others make do with much less. Teach them that everything from their school to the breakfast you make for them is something to be appreciated and grateful for.

arrogance

(AIR-uh-gens)

noun

A feeling of self-importance that may cause one to treat people casually or with contempt.

The fact that the new boy didn't think he needed any help was an example of his ARROGANCE.

Children can appear arrogant from time to time, and it's not unusual for them to put their needs before others. This is a habit that is best broken as early as possible. Arrogance sets your child up for failure because arrogant people alienate others, overestimate their abilities, and are generally unpleasant to be around. Teach your children that they are not alone in this world. They must happily coexist with their family members, friends, and classmates—which means being open to the needs of others and putting themselves second at times.

art

(art)

noun

A work of beauty, often associated with music, painting, or writing.

My birthday cake was so beautiful you could say it was a work of ART.

Music, architecture, drawings, photographs, paintings, and great works of literature make our world a much better place to live in. They add beauty, grace, and hope to our lives. It's important to teach your children to respect and admire art, but while it's wonderful to take your child to a local gallery, concert, or museum, these trips aren't the only way to necessarily create appreciation. Talk to your children about what you think is beautiful. Make a point of observing good architecture in your community. Take photographs together. Check out art books from the library. Your children will soon see that art is not limited to museums, but rather is something that they can find everywhere.

attention

(uh-TEN-shun)

noun

The ability to focus on details or provide the appropriate care that something requires.

My younger sister loves it when I pay ATTENTION to her.

Attention can feel like a loaded word for a parent. It seems as if your children require constant attention . . . yet it can be nearly impossible for them to pay attention to anything. Talk to your child about the benefits of paying attention. Show him how happy he can make younger siblings or even the family pets by taking time to give them some attention. You can also show him what can happen when he pays attention to details. Point out something special in your garden or an interesting detail in an illustration of a beloved book. Eventually, paying attention will seem like something that's fun to do rather than a dull, tiresome requirement.

balance

(BAL-ens)

noun

Steadiness of emotional and mental health, especially under stress or daily demands, or the art of maintaining the stability between two different factors of equal importance.

It can be hard to maintain a BALANCE between the fun of playing sports and the challenge of homework.

Maintaining balance in your life is probably a constant struggle. Just as soon as you've mastered it, something else is tossed on your plate. While adults are very familiar with this struggle, children are also struggling to find a balance in their lives. With school pressure, activities, and homework to complete, many kids are finding it difficult to find the time to do everything. You can help your children find balance by not letting them overschedule themselves. Also be sure to let them know that things occasionally fall through the cracks—but all is usually well in the end.

beauty

(BYOO-tee)

noun

The quality in a person or thing that pleases either the mind or the senses.

The BEAUTY of springtime flowers makes my day brighter.

It's never been more challenging to remember that we are surrounded by beauty. Perfectly sculpted celebrities and dazzling material objects often trump the beauty of green grass, summer's first rose, or your child's expression as she is falling asleep. By taking the time to remember what's beautiful to you, you'll be well poised to teach your children that they don't have to look far or spend money to experience beauty. Be vocal about your love of nature, friends, family, art, and design. Your children will take cues from you and will quickly learn that beauty is always within arm's reach.

belief

(bee-LEEF)

noun

A conviction in the truth or correctness of an idea, statement, or ideology.

It was my mom's BELIEF that I could excel at art that made me comfortable taking the class.

Children are fortunate in that they get to enjoy many different beliefs. They get to believe in the existence of many wonderful things: mermaids, superheroes, and even that the tooth fairy leaves them money when they lose a tooth. While it's fine to let your children enjoy these fantasies, it's also essential to teach them how important it is to believe that their friends and family will always be there for them. Tell your child that you believe her abilities will help her grow into a wonderful person who will make the world a better place.

benevolence

(buh-NEV-uh-lens)

noun

The tendency/habit of doing something simply to be kind or helpful.

That my aunt wanted nothing in return for all the help she gave the family is another example of her BENEVOLENCE.

Adults understand that a benevolent act comes with its own rewards and that helping or giving out of the goodness of your heart can leave you feeling incredibly happy. It can be a challenge to teach a child that giving and expecting nothing in return is a rewarding experience. Remind your children that there are many people in their lives who do kind acts for them without expecting something back. Teachers, caregivers, and family act out of love. Encourage your children to try doing something kind for a family member or friend, even if just to experience how happy spreading joy can make them.

bliss

(bliss)

noun

A feeling of perfect happiness or joy.

Swimming with my friends on a hot summer day is pure BLISS.

Adults don't get to experience sheer, unadulterated bliss very often. To fully escape from the stress and distraction of your hectic life may seem to require a long tropical vacation. Unlike adults, bliss comes naturally to children as they jump, run, or simply play with friends. While it's easy for your child to associate bliss with birthdays, holidays, and other special events, make sure he learns to appreciate and enjoy all of the blissful moments life has to offer. Encourage him to notice his bliss while doing the everyday things that make him happy, like sports, reading, crafts, and family time. If your child understands that bliss is always within reach, he will be well on his way to being happy and well-adjusted.

calm

(kallm)

noun

A moment of total peace and quiet that is also free of anxiety.

I am always sure to enjoy a moment of CALM before a piano recital.

Calm is not a word that would accurately describe most households with children; noise and action follow children wherever they go. For you to be a good parent, you need to experience complete calm from time to time. Explain to your child that everyone needs to have an occasional moment of peace and quiet. Set time aside, even if only a short while, where your children are obligated to behave in a calm and peaceful manner. While this may sound easier said than done, you could be surprised to find that quiet time will become a habit that sticks.

capable

(KAY-puh-bull)

adjective

Being especially good at a task or skill.

I took lots of lessons, and as a result I'm a very CAPABLE swimmer.

Feeling capable is a wonderful quality; it makes life easier to know that you're able to handle whatever is thrown at you. And while you may tend to praise your child for being capable in certain areas—whether it be math, karate, swimming, or singing—it's helpful to instill an overall feeling of capability within him. Tell him that, while it's great that he has specific capabilities, it's his intelligence, integrity, and kindness that make him capable as a person overall. This will put him in a good position to deal with whatever challenges he is faced with in the future.

celebrate

(SELL-uh-brate)

verb

To mark a special occasion or positive event with festive activities.

My family is always happy to CELEBRATE when I bring home a good report card.

Children know that birthdays and major holidays—Christmas, Easter, Thanksgiving, Hanukkah, Passover, and even Halloween—are cause for celebration. It's also easy for children to think that for a celebration to take place, elaborate plans need to be made, presents need to be purchased, and guests need to be invited. There are many moments in life to celebrate—learning to read, a week of good behavior, the last or first day of school—so make a habit of celebrating in small ways, like whipping up a special dessert or taking a simple trip to the park together.

challenge

(CHAL-enj)

noun

A test of your abilities in a complicated, stimulating situation or environment.

I enjoyed the CHALLENGE of learning to play the flute in my school orchestra.

It's easy for children to think of the word "challenge" in a negative way. Children are always in the position of learning new things and, when a task or situation becomes complicated, they have a tendency to become frightened or get frustrated. Your child may want you to intervene and help when she is faced with a challenge. While it may be tempting to do so, reassure your child that challenges, while sometimes scary, can ultimately be fun and exciting. Remind her that if she didn't face challenges, she wouldn't be able to try new sports, read new books, or even start at a new school—all activities she likely enjoys!

character

(KARE-eck-ter)

noun

A person's true nature, made up of traits such as kindness, intelligence, and integrity.

As her CHARACTER suggested, Ms. Smith turned out to be completely reliable.

Unfortunately we don't spend much time talking about a person's character these days. Of course you want to surround yourself with people who are kind and reliable—but it's easy to get distracted by other qualities, such as fun and excitement. Teach your children that while it's important to be amused by their friends, it's also important that they surround themselves with people of good character. Talk to your children about what qualities they value in their friends, and encourage them to exhibit those characteristics themselves.

charity

(CHARE-ih-tee)

noun

A willingness to help those in need with money, possessions, or time; the act of viewing people in a kind or favorable way.

My sense of CHARITY kept me from assuming that the new girl at school was stuck-up for not talking to anyone at lunch.

While everyone should try to give what they can to causes that they feel are worthy, it is important to remember that charity extends beyond the act of giving. It is easy to make snap judgments, and children are often not equipped to understand why some people may be acting a certain way. By teaching them about charity, and how they should refuse to judge others, they will learn that there's often more to a person than meets the eye.

choice

(choyce)

noun

The decision to select one thing or course of action over another.

I made a good, healthy CHOICE when I ate an apple instead of a cookie.

Adults know that the choices they make on a daily basis directly impact the quality of their lives. Adults know the difference between right and wrong and, under normal circumstances, don't need to spend much time deciding what to do. Children are still learning how to make good choices. They are just beginning to learn that, on a certain level, they can determine the outcome of things by making a good or bad choice. Talk to your child about the choices he makes. Why was hitting his sister a bad choice? Was doing his homework right after school a good choice? By having these discussions, you'll be making it easier for your child to make better decisions.

classic

(KLASS-ick)

adjective

Of the best quality; maintaining everlasting value.

My mom has CLASSIC style. She buys good clothes that will never look dated.

Children can get away with quite a bit when it comes to style. Mismatched clothing, a princess costume, or a quirky hat makes them even more adorable. While children don't necessarily need to concern themselves with classic style at a young age, it can be beneficial to talk to them about what makes something classic. Talk to them about certain choices you've made when it comes to decorating your home or building your wardrobe. Explain why certain books, songs, and movies have stood the test of time. By exposing your child to classics— whether in literature, film, or art—you'll sow the seeds for a lifetime of appreciation of the finer things.

clean

(kleen)

adjective

Free from impurities.

When we moved into our house, our basement wasn't CLEAN.

Clean is probably not a word your children like to hear. The second a kid hears the word "clean" her mind likely immediately goes to bath time, or picking up all of her toys. It's important for children to understand that clean is a concept that extends beyond the state of their bedroom. Living in a clean environment means having respect for the place you live, work, or go to school. Teach your children to put trash where it belongs, and to recycle whenever possible. Not only is it crucial that your children live in a clean home, but they must also learn to take care of the earth and oceans as well.

comfort

(KUM-furt)

noun

A feeling of physical ease or emotional security.

Nothing says COMFORT to me like slipping into a bed with crisp, clean sheets.

Children are accustomed to receiving comfort from their parents. After all, it's usually mom or dad who covers a child with a well-worn blanket, brings his teddy bear into his room at bedtime, or makes his favorite foods when he is sick. But as a child grows older, that teddy bear likely won't provide as much comfort as it used to, so share some of the things that bring you comfort with your children. Watch a happy movie together, play lively music, cuddle with the family pet. Soon your children will learn to find new objects of comfort all on their own.

commitment

(kuh-MITT-ment)

noun

Absolute dedication to a person, relationship, cause, or idea.

My father's COMMITMENT to ensuring we have a good education is inspiring.

Commitment might seem like a word that doesn't easily fit into the life of a young person, as it's easiest to associate the concept with adult relationships, family, and careers. However, understanding the concept of commitment can give your child a better grasp of what it takes to excel in certain areas. It takes commitment to excel in school or play a team sport. Your child may also want to commit to reaching certain goals, like saving up enough money to buy a skateboard or take a trip. Sharing the lengths that you'll go to to keep your commitments will show your children that it takes strength, courage, and direction to get where they want to go as well.

community

(kuh-MYOO-nih-tee)

noun

A group of people who exist together in the same area or share a common interest.

The COMMUNITY I live in is warm, welcoming, and diverse.

Most people don't live on their own and your family likely lives as part of a larger community, whether it be a neighborhood within a big city, a quiet suburban block, or a small town. Regardless of what kind of community you live in, it's important that your children understand that you share the space you live in with other people and how the people behave collectively determines the quality of your community. Encourage your children to be polite to neighbors, not to make unnecessary noise, to put trash in appropriate places, and to do whatever they can to make their community more pleasant for everyone.

companionship

(kum-PAN-yun-ship)

noun

The relationship you share with a close friend or loved one.

I would be lost without the COMPANIONSHIP of my friends and neighbors.

When you need help, someone to talk to, a favor, or to just have fun, you likely call on a special friend. There is nothing better than the companionship of someone who has been by your side for what feels like forever and truly knows you. Your children probably know who your special companions are, and have grown up watching you laugh and cry together. Let your children know how much you value this relationship—and help them understand that having such a close companion is like having an extra family member because that person is someone you can always count on, are always happy to see, and who will be by your side for the long run.

comparison

(kum-PAR-ih-sun)

noun

An examination of the differences between two people or objects.

The COMPARISION that my friend made of my sister and me hurt my feelings.

Adults know that comparing yourself to others leads to bad feelings. It's so easy to feel badly about what you perceive others have that you don't. Teach your children that comparing themselves to others is not a good way to spend mental energy. Everyone is different, is graced with different gifts, and needs to appreciate what they have in life. Let your children know that while we might assume others are happy or healthy, sometimes another person's life is not as easy as it may seem on the surface.

compatible

(kum-PAT-uh-bull)

adjective

Being able to live, work, or spend time together without experiencing much conflict.

My friends and I are very COMPATIBLE, we rarely argue or fight.

It is wonderful for parents to watch their child interact with someone she is truly compatible with. Friendships that run smoothly and are free of arguments or differences can be rare—especially for kids. It's hard for a child to understand that she might have to struggle to get along well with certain people. While it's good to encourage your child to get along with others in all circumstances, it's also okay to explain that not all people are compatible. If your child is struggling to make a friendship work with a particular person, let her know that this doesn't mean that she's done anything wrong.

complicated

(KOMM-plih-kay-tid)

adjective

Difficult, due to a need to incorporate different ideas, concepts, or opinions.

We had to take everyone's needs into account, so deciding where to go on vacation was COMPLICATED.

Parents are not strangers to complicated situations; they have to figure out how to balance day care, work demands, and school schedules and it's always frustrating when an additional complicated situation is thrown on top of everything they already have to deal with. However, the challenges of parenthood prepare you well for managing complications. When your child is faced with his first complicated situation—either at home or at school—be open about how difficult such situations can be, but show how they can be managed with careful thinking and finesse.

composure

(kum-POE-zhur)

noun

The ability to maintain calm and steady control in an emotional situation.

I was so angry that we lost the game that it was hard for me to maintain my COMPOSURE.

Sometimes it can be easy to envy children, as they aren't always expected to be quiet and composed, at least not when very young. Although you would certainly prefer that your kids keep their composure in the face of disappointments or challenges, you are probably not surprised when they are too upset to do so. However, as your children grow older, it will help them tremendously to know how to keep their emotions in check. There are countless situations in life when people would like to scream or throw things in frustration. Tell your children that this behavior is unacceptable, and explain that people who can't maintain their composure face additional struggles in life simply because they can't hold onto their self-control.

compromise

(KOMM-pruh-myz)

verb

To settle a disagreement by accepting something different than what you originally wanted.

I really wanted to play in the park after dinner, but I had to COMPROMISE and agree to play in the backyard.

Parents often feel as though they are constantly negotiating with their children. And while you want your children to understand that "no" means "no," sometimes there are compromises that are worth making. Adults know that life is full of compromise, and it will be helpful for your child to understand that while he may not always get exactly what he wants, there are often other desirable outcomes to certain situations. When your child desperately wants you to take him to the park but you're just too busy, take the time to offer an alternative solution. Will he be happy playing a board game with you? Or throwing a ball in the backyard? The ability of your child to understand and accept compromise will ultimately make both of your lives easier.

confidence

(KON-fih-dens)

noun

The belief that you or someone else is fully capable of accomplishing a task.

I didn't think I would do well at the swim meet, but my mom had CONFIDENCE that I would.

There isn't a quality that sets a child up for success more surely than confidence. Feeling that she is capable of facing challenges, succeeding at school and work, and being confident in her interactions with people undoubtedly makes your child's life easier. The best way to demonstrate confidence to your child is to be confident yourself. Continue to develop your own sense of self-assurance in your actions with others and how you face various challenges. Let your child know that even if a task is difficult, your confidence in yourself keeps you from stepping back or being afraid.

conscience

(KON-shens)

noun

The part of your mind that dictates your behavior and helps decide what actions are right or wrong.

My CONSCIENCE told me that it was okay to tell a small white lie. I didn't want my aunt to know I didn't like my birthday present.

While most children are innately aware that they have a conscience, it's unlikely that they actually understand what it is. Even so, you may have experienced your child behaving in a guilty manner, or feeling sad after doing something wrong—even if you haven't yet scolded her. Explain to your child that when she does something that she knows deep down is wrong, she'll trigger a negative feeling that is her conscience speaking to her. Ideally your child will eventually learn to master her worst impulses before she creates a guilty conscience.

consequence

(KON-sih-kwens)

noun

Something that occurs as a result of a previous action.

The CONSEQUENCE of me not listening to my mother was that I didn't get to watch any TV before bed.

Adults are well aware of the consequences that will occur if they don't do what's necessary. You could face consequences as drastic as losing your job if you don't perform well, or as minor as missing out on a good night's sleep if you need to stay up late to take care of unfinished tasks. The sooner your child can understand the relationship between his actions and the consequences that result from them, the sooner he will learn to control his behavior. Make sure that your child understands the consequences of not doing his homework (bad grades), not brushing his teeth (cavities), and not being a good friend (losing a friendship). Hopefully, being aware of consequences will encourage your child to make good choices.

consideration

(kun-sid-ur-AY-shun)

noun

The quality of maintaining concern for and sensitivity to the feelings of other people.

I will have to give careful CONSIDERATION to what we do to celebrate my mom's birthday.

Consideration is a highly valued quality in a friend or family member—it feels great to know that another person is looking out for your feelings. However, consideration is a concept that can take a child a while to grasp, as it's natural for kids to be more concerned with having their immediate needs met than thinking about how others feel. Show your child how consideration has a direct impact on the quality of her life. Remind her how happy it makes a friend if she agrees to do what the friend wants to do, even for a short while. Your child will soon learn that when she is considerate to others, others are more likely to be considerate to her.

consistency

(kun-SISS-ten-see)

noun

The ability to maintain a particular standard of behavior or to do a task repeatedly with similar results.

Even though it's difficult, I try to maintain the same level of CONSISTENCY in my schoolwork.

It can be tempting to take shortcuts; after all, it's easy to think that people don't pay attention to the level of our work or how we conduct ourselves. But you know that taking the easy route often complicates things. By being consistent in your behavior, you'll show your child that, while this may take more effort, it's how you're able to produce quality work and maintain healthy relationships. While consistency may be a hard concept for children to execute, they'll soon begin to understand its value as they receive praise for consistently doing a weekly chore or making a habit of bringing backyard flowers to an elderly neighbor.

conversation

(kon-ver-SAY-shun)

noun

The art of talking to another person casually about thoughts, opinions, ideas, or feelings.

I enjoyed all of the CONVERSATIONS I had with the other guests at my friend's birthday party.

Sometimes it seems as if people no longer talk to each other. It's easier to send a text or an e-mail, and it almost feels strange to actually talk to someone on the phone. While all of these new ways to communicate are wonderful, make sure that your child also knows how to hold an actual conversation. Talking to adults may be intimidating, but with practice children will soon learn that it's not so different from talking to their friends at school. Encourage them to ask your friends, relatives, and houseguests how they're feeling and what they've been up to—and let your kids know that it's okay to answer questions, too.

conviction

(kun-VICK-shun)

noun

A strong belief or opinion that a person maintains regardless of the circumstances.

It's my mom's CONVICTION that everyone should get a second chance.

Sometimes it seems that the only convictions children have relate to what time bedtime should be or what they consider to be an acceptable dinner. If you want your children to develop a strong moral core and share your values, talk to them about your convictions. Explain that there are certain issues where your feelings are unwavering. You hold these convictions because your values are a strong part of who you are. Eventually your children will begin to understand that having a strong feeling is one thing but the commitment to hold on to it and see it through is another.

creativity

(kree-ay-TIV-ih-tee)

noun

The ability to develop original and unique ideas or physical accomplishments.

The beautiful mural on our bedroom wall is another example of my sister's CREATIVITY.

Everyone associates the concept of creativity with children, as they have a unique ability to draw, design, build, and play totally unencumbered. It's unfortunate that many of us lose this ability as we grow older. By encouraging your children to appreciate and enjoy their creativity, you're showing them that this is a characteristic that can be brought into adulthood. Creativity isn't limited to art and design; it extends to how you choose to approach a problem or situation. By holding on to their creativity, your children can grow into excellent problem solvers, thinkers, and planners.

cruelty

(KROO-uhl-tee)

noun

Act or speech meant to cause distress and pain to another person or creature.

The CRUELTY inflicted on the new classmate was wrong and upsetting.

Every parent hopes that their children will never encounter cruelty. However, the reality is that you can't always protect your children from the cruel actions of others. In this age of bullying, it may be helpful for your child to understand what cruelty actually is. Let them know that purposely causing pain to another person or creature—whether verbally or physically—is totally unacceptable. They should know that they never have to tolerate any cruel behavior that may be inflicted upon them. Talk to them about how to handle a situation where they feel that they or someone else is being hurt purposely.

daring

(DAIR-ing)

adjective

Unconventional and bold, putting someone ahead of the pack. ˙

I enjoy wearing DARING clothing. I don't like to dress like everyone else.

When you think about people who stand out from the crowd—those who are innovative and brilliant—you'll likely see that they are daring in some way. People who can move forward with their ideas without worrying that others will judge them have made strides in art, technology, medicine, fashion, and politics. Teach your child that it's okay to think differently; encourage her to stick to her ideas and have the strength to execute them. While people may not initially agree with your child's bold ideas, it's likely that others will eventually admire your child for her innovation.

daydream

(DAY-dreem)

noun

A distracting but pleasant thought or fantasy.

I laid around on Sunday afternoon enjoying my DAYDREAM.

Life is busy—even for children. Between school, homework, and extracurricular activities, kids rarely have time to relax, be silly, or have a single thought of their own, while adults often try to prevent themselves from getting distracted by random thoughts, even pleasant ones. By allowing yourself to daydream, you'll teach your child that it's okay to take a break from the craziness of life. Daydreaming encourages imagination, helps recharge you, and can even promote creativity. Let your child know that daydreaming isn't just a silly way to spend time, but a healthy, useful tool that will serve him well throughout his life.

dedication

(dedd-ih-KAY-shun)

noun

A strong commitment or devotion to another person, cause, or activity.

My mom's DEDICATION to maintaining a clean, warm, and loving household is very admirable.

One day your child desperately wants to be a ballerina, the next day a firefighter. It's natural for children to change their minds about what interests them. However, be sure to instill a sense that hard work and dedication are the keys to getting ahead in a particular area. While your daughter may not be ready to commit to ballet, make sure she understands that having dedication allows people to reach their goals. When your child finds an activity that she is passionate about, encourage her to stick with it and see where her dedication takes her.

defend

(dee-FEND)

verb

To protect somebody from harm, or to speak on their behalf when they need help.

I knew my friend wasn't responsible for the mess, so I spoke up to DEFEND him.

Today's children have to face some difficult challenges. Bullying is at an all-time high, and no parent wants his child to be faced with bullying. While you can talk to your children about how they should respond if bullied, also consider talking to them about what they should do if someone else is being bullied. Let them know that it's good to defend someone who's being victimized. While you should emphasize to your children that you don't want them to get involved physically, they can and should make a point of standing up for a person who isn't being treated right. Having the courage to stand up to an injustice, even if it's just on the playground, will build character and confidence.

dependable

(dee-PEN-duh-bull)

adjective

Characteristically trustworthy and responsible; can be relied on.

I get lots of babysitting jobs because I've proven that I'm DEPENDABLE.

While being dependable doesn't sound like the most exciting quality, it is an essential part of being able to succeed in the workplace, fulfilling our responsibilities at home, and maintaining good friendships. Let your child know that you depend on him. It's crucial to the happiness of your household that your child can be depended on to get ready for school, finish his homework, pick up his toys, and go to bed on time. Be sure your child understands that if he's not dependable, it has a negative impact on everything from where he's invited to what kind of responsibilities he's given.

deserving

(dih-ZUR-ving)

adjective

Having earned something through hard work or good behavior.

My mom took me shopping because she felt I was DESERVING of a new toy.

Parents adore their children so much that it can be incredibly difficult to say "No." It's also easier to give in to a wish than to deal with the complaining that usually accompanies the denial of most requests. But receiving a special present because she deserves it makes the experience all the more significant to your child. When your child expresses interest in going to a particular place or in owning a new toy or game, tell her that you'd be happy to give her what she desires when she's done something to "deserve" it. Be sure to spell out what would constitute deserving behavior in your mind. By teaching your child that good behavior deserves a reward and that special treats are all the more special for being earned, you are imparting two useful lessons.

design

(dih-ZYNE)

noun

The construction or appearance of an object.

I love the DESIGN of the necklace my parents gave me for my birthday.

Children have an innate sense of design. They are drawn to vibrant colors, love unusual patterns, and are delighted by new textures. Sometimes parents have to be practical, and thoughts about good design have to be pushed aside, but to teach your children about good design and beauty, vow to make conscious choices about what you bring into your home. Don't just decorate your surroundings with practical items. Be sure to add certain pieces that you find beautiful, even with your kids in the house. Allow your kids to participate in design choices by letting them select a paint color or decorate their walls with their own artwork.

detail

(DEE-tale)

noun

Refinements or decoration, usually something that is insignificant on its own but important as part of a whole.

I wasn't that excited about my new room until my mom added that one special DETAIL that made it beautiful.

The world would be a dull place if it weren't for all of the details that make it so special. You take the time to add the personal touches that make your home unique—you decorate birthday cakes, dress carefully, and prepare food in a way that pleases your family. Encourage your children to add their own flourishes to whatever they do. While it's important that they still follow rules when necessary, let them know that they can add personal details to their bedrooms or a school assignment when appropriate. By encouraging them to play with the details, you'll help them express their personalities and develop a stronger sense of self.

difference

(DIFF-er-ens)

noun

A unique trait or feature that distinguishes people or things from one another.

The main DIFFERENCE between my sister and me is that I don't care for sports.

Perhaps one of the most wonderful qualities that children possess is the fact that they are generally unaware of the differences in people. Children barely notice differences in skin color and aren't fazed by the compositions of different types of families. Instead, they judge their friends based on how much they enjoy their company. Make a point of encouraging your child to hold on to these qualities. Be open-minded, and let your child be your guide. If the fact that a good friend has two moms rather than a mom and a dad doesn't bother your child, don't let it bother you. If more people held on to this childlike nonjudgmental quality, the world might be a more peaceful place. As your child grows older, continue to remind her that differences make things more interesting and people unique. The atmosphere of a friend's house, the way it's decorated, and even the foods her friend eats are not differences to be feared, but rather examples of what makes that family unique.

disappointment

(dis-uh-POYNT-ment)

noun

The feeling you experience when your hopes, dreams, and wants are not realized.

We couldn't go on a vacation this year, which was a big DIS-APPOINTMENT for all of us.

No parents want their children to experience disappointment. It's natural to want to give them all you can and protect them from every possible disappointment. Disappointment is unfortunately a fact of life, and the faster you can teach your child to accept and bounce back from disappointments, the stronger he will be. Managing his disappointment at not being able to attend a birthday party when young may translate later in life to greater resilience when he is unable to get into his first-choice college or get a promotion he feels he deserves.

discover

(diss-CUV-ur)

verb

To find out or learn about something that was previously unknown.

I was so happy to DISCOVER that there was a secret cubby in the back of my bedroom closet.

Watching a child make discoveries is delightful for a parent. You never forget the first time you took your child to the beach, for a ride on a carousel, or for her first ice cream cone. While it's a parent's job to introduce his or her children to new concepts, be sure that you also encourage their spirit of discovery. What will your child discover on her own? Take her to a city or park and let her dictate the day's activities. Let her make a mess of her toys in your living room and see what kinds of creations she comes up with. Being comfortable with discovering new things leads to confidence, creativity, and a healthy imagination.

diversity

(dih-VUR-suh-tee)

noun

The variety that exists among a group of people.

The DIVERSITY of my school was a big draw to my parents.

The world is a diverse place. In addition to ethnic diversity, there's socioeconomic and cultural diversity . . . all of which make the world much more interesting. At some point, your child will begin to notice differences between people, either at his school or within your community. Explain that diversity is what makes your neighborhood or school vibrant and that differences are not to be feared, but embraced. It may help your children to know that they are free to ask questions. They'll soon see that, despite some minor differences, most people are in fact quite similar and have much in common with your own family.

doubt

(dowt)

verb

To feel unsure of something or someone.

I sometimes DOUBT that I will be able to understand what my teacher is explaining to me.

As an adult, you are accustomed to feeling doubt, whether it is related to something you are hoping will happen or whether you are mistrustful of a person's actions. You also know that it isn't unusual for your doubt to be completely unfounded. Children often feel doubt, but don't understand that this is a common feeling that everyone experiences. Help your child understand that doubt is normal. It isn't possible to feel confident all of the time. Show your child that doubt can also be helpful and explain that sometimes you doubt another person for a good reason.

dream

(dreem)

noun

Something that you long for and daydream about frequently, usually something that feels unlikely to materialize.

I love Paris, so it's been a DREAM of mine to live in France.

Everyone has experienced the joy of having a dream come true, as well as the disappointment that must be faced when it's clear that a dream will not be realized. While all parents want their children to have hopes and dreams, how do you learn to support those dreams that might happen and let your children know that some are not realistic? If your child's dream is to achieve something that is a long shot, but within the realm of possibility, do what you can to support her. If you feel the dream is incredibly unlikely, just remind yourself that many dreams eventually fade over time. Your child will move on. Nevertheless, dreams are an essential part to growing and developing as a person. Your child's dreams will lead to goals and—whether the dream is realistic or not—it's important for her to have something to strive for.

education

(edj-uh-KAY-shun)

noun

Studying or schooling that develops skills and imparts valuable information.

I don't always want to go to school, but my EDUCATION is the key to my getting ahead in life.

While your child may be an excellent student or athlete, or may have lots of friends at his school, there are always times when he would rather just stay home and play or relax. It helps to remember that just about everyone feels this way at some point. Getting an education is a commitment and a challenge, which is why it can be fun to do something other than homework sometimes. Reminding your child that school is often fun, and balancing his education with stimulating and exciting activities will help instill in him a love of education that will guide him successfully into adulthood.

embrace

(em-BRAYCE)

verb

To take a welcoming approach to a belief, lifestyle, or another person.

My family has really EMBRACED the concept of healthy living.

It's exciting to find a concept or idea that moves you. When you discover something new—like a form of exercise, a new style of cooking, or a hobby—it's normal to want to truly embrace it and make it a part of your everyday existence. While children tend to get excited about a variety of different things, it sometimes takes encouragement for them to embrace a new idea after the initial novelty passes. If your child develops a curiosity about history, tailor some activities to cultivate her interest. If she's interested in art, make a point of taking her to a museum and talking about the works you see. By encouraging your child to embrace something new, you may be setting her on the path toward developing a lifelong passion.

emotion

(ee-MOE-shun)

noun

A variety of spontaneous feelings or mental reactions to conditions or events.

The EMOTION I felt after winning the contest was overwhelming.

Adults don't always understand their emotions. Sometimes you can be confused about why a particular situation makes you so happy or nearly brings you to tears, and if adults can't always be in touch with their emotions, children shouldn't be expected to, either. Just because a child can feel an emotion doesn't mean he understands why he's having it or whether it's an appropriate response. Make a point of asking your child why he's mad, or what it was about a situation that made him so happy. After talking through his feelings, your child will begin to have a greater understanding of what he is feeling and why.

empathy

(EM-puh-thee)

noun

The ability to directly identify with another person's problems or challenges.

My dog had died recently, so I had EMPATHY for my friend's situation.

When you are suffering through a difficult time, it can help tremendously to know that someone has empathy for your situation. Knowing someone else has had a similar experience helps you to know that you're not alone. Understanding the concept of empathy can start early, so encourage your child to relate and empathize when a friend is upset about being homesick or scared of something. Having empathy will not only help your child create strong friendships, it will also begin to help her understand that she is not alone when she is troubled.

entitlement

(en-TIE-tul-ment)

noun

The right to receive something, such as a job or material item.

....

It's okay to feel a sense of ENTITLEMENT if you've worked hard and deserve what you hope to get.

....

Many parents worry that their children will grow up with an inappropriate sense of entitlement. After you've worked hard to make it through school and establish your career and your home, it can be frustrating to feel that your children have expectations about what is due to them. While it's fine for your children to expect to receive what they deserve, make a point of explaining that entitlement is a result of hard work. Without earning the right to a job or money, the satisfaction that comes with receiving it isn't nearly as great.

environment

(en-VIE-ren-ment; en-VIE-ern-ment)

noun

The conditions that surround you, your family, and your friends; your immediate surroundings as well as the natural world.

I love the calm, peaceful ENVIRONMENT of my home.

Most parents want their children to know that being wasteful is harmful to the natural world, and it's crucial that your children understand how their actions affect the environment. Explain to them why you recycle as much as possible and try to conserve energy when you can. Your children's immediate environment is important, too. Tell them that their actions—helping to clean and organize, and being conscious about what's brought into the home—also have an impact on their quality of living. A peaceful immediate environment for sleeping, eating, reading, and playing is an essential part of a healthy existence.

envy

(EN-vee)

verb

To feel discomfort that stems from wanting a possession or a quality that someone else has.

I really ENVY my friend who can sing and dance better than I can.

It's nearly impossible not to feel envy at certain times. It's easy to think that other people have it better than you do—they have more money, a better job, and a bigger house. However, other people might be envious of how you speak your mind or bake incredible pies. Adults know that comparing their life to someone else's is a waste of energy, and also know that they see only part of the picture of others' lives. It's important to teach your children that, while it's easy to envy what someone else has, it's better for them to appreciate what they have going for themselves, and also that it's hard to know the challenges that other people are actually facing.

evocative

(ee-VOCK-uh-tiv)

adjective

Tending to create strong or vivid memories or reminders of things not present.

Even though it's the middle of winter, the blue sky and crisp air are EVOCATIVE of springtime.

It's probably unusual for children to feel that anything is evocative of a time from their past; however, it can be interesting for children to know about things that are evocative to their parents. When something reminds you of your childhood— such as a vintage bicycle, an ice cream truck, or maybe an old cartoon—use this as an opportunity to share memories from your youth with your child. Listening to what your childhood was like is a wonderful way for your children to develop an understanding of your past and to grow closer to you.

example

(ig-ZAM-pull)

noun

A person you view as someone you can model yourself after.

My uncle is the best EXAMPLE of a hardworking person that I have ever met.

It can be a challenge for a parent to provide a constant example of how to behave. It's a lot to try to instill manners, sincerity, honesty, and kindness into your child's personality all at once. When the pressure of being a role model is too much, don't hesitate to think about who else can set a great example for your kids. Talk to your children about the qualities you admire in other family members and friends. If, for instance, your brother provides an especially good example of how to treat other people, point this out to your kids. They will notice these traits and will see how they make your brother an especially good and likeable person.

excellence

(ECK-suh-lens)

noun

The quality that makes a person or thing especially outstanding.

I strive for EXCELLENCE in many areas of my life—my studies, soccer, and being a good daughter and friend.

Parents want their children to achieve excellence in a variety of areas. You'd like them to get good grades, and excel at a sport, activity, or musical instrument. But don't expect excellence too soon. While it's important to nurture a child's talent, remember that it can take years to reach the level that qualifies as excellent. For example, becoming a truly excellent piano player or dancer takes time, dedication, and commitment. Know that it will take continued encouragement and support from you. If your child understands what makes something excellent, she'll see that there is an additional level for her to strive for, whether academically, in sports, or in another passion that she is pursuing wholeheartedly.

expectation

(eck-speck-TAY-shun)

noun

Confidence that a certain event will take place or that a person will behave in a particular way.

My parents' EXPECTATION was that I would perform well on the test.

Parenthood is a delicate balancing act requiring constant attention, and adults are keenly aware of the expectations they have to live up to. Children, on the other hand, are unlikely to know what's expected of them unless it's made clear. What do you expect from your children in terms of behavior, school, and help around the house? Tell your children that your family depends on them to accomplish certain tasks and to maintain a particular level of behavior. Knowing that making their beds, taking out the garbage, or coming to dinner without being asked twice affects the entire family will make these tasks seem important.

experience

(ick-SPEER-ee-ens)

noun

An event or activity that helps you develop skills and knowledge in a particular area; the skills and knowledge themselves.

Traveling to another country with my family was a great EXPERIENCE.

You know by now that one of the best ways to learn about something new or increase your knowledge of a particular area is to allow yourself to have more experiences. However, children are not always excited about the prospect of having new experiences, which can be overwhelming and intimidating. Be sure to point out that we discover where our skills lie, and what brings us pleasure, by opening ourselves up to new experiences. Encourage your child to see a new experience as an adventure. If she is still feeling reluctant about trying something new, offer to accompany her or to try something new together.

expert

(ECK-spurt)

noun

A person who possesses tremendous skill or a great deal of knowledge about a certain subject.

The curator we met on our school field trip is an EXPERT in impressionist art.

While adults know how long and hard a person has to work to become an expert at anything, children tend to get excited about an activity and then become frustrated when they don't master it almost immediately. Talk to your child about how to develop his passions . . . what steps can he take to make progress and excel? Explain that the person who is teaching him or the person he admires in this particular field is an expert who has spent years honing her craft. Remind your child of this whenever he becomes discouraged.

explore

(ick-SPLORE)

verb

To aim to discover by traveling elsewhere or examining your immediate surroundings.

We love the sights and sounds when we visit the city, and never fail to discover exciting new places that we want to EXPLORE.

Children were born to explore. The grass and trees growing in your backyard and the sights seen out of the car window as you drive through the city provide an endless landscape for a child to discover. Take the time to explore your park, your neighborhood, museums, and even the local shops and restaurants with your child. By teaching her to appreciate all the excitement that can be found in your immediate surroundings, you'll be showing her that the world is full of great opportunities and wonderful things to experience. All she has to do is make a point of seeking them out.

extravagance

(eck-STRAV-uh-gens)

noun

A dramatic, excessive, and sometimes wasteful spending of money.

The EXTRAVAGANCE of the birthday party seemed like overkill to all invited.

It's certainly okay to be extravagant from time to time. It's exciting to do something out of the ordinary, like spend a large amount of money on dinner in a restaurant or on a piece of furniture for your home. However, extravagance can easily go from special to ordinary if it's a regular occurrence. If a child is constantly lavished with expensive items, those items no longer seem extraordinary, but become expected. Teach your children that true extravagance is to be reserved for special moments and occasions, and that they should enjoy every such moment to the fullest.

fact

(fackt)

noun

Information or knowledge that has been proven to be truthful.

It is a well-known FACT that the United States was founded on July 4, 1776.

Information is everywhere, but how do you teach your children to differentiate between accurate information and false information when they can access so much so easily? Make sure your children understand that a fact is different from an idea, theory, or hypothesis. Teach them that facts are undisputed, and come from reputable sources. Facts are not limited to the world of science, but are also found in history, geography, math, and even in what your children know to have actually occurred in everyday life. Having an understanding of what makes something a fact can establish a foundation of knowledge that your child can continue to build upon as he grows.

faith

(fayth)

noun

A strong belief and devotion to something without actually having proof that it exists.

Even though bad things sometimes happen where I live, I continue to have FAITH in my community and in those who live in it.

Parents can find themselves in the position of explaining to their children that many fears and anxieties are only in their heads—for instance, that the monster they imagine lives in their closet doesn't actually exist. The job of explaining faith can be a real challenge. Whether you place faith in God or your family, let your child know that faith is a feeling—and feelings can't be seen. Assuring your child that you will always be there for him or that his brother will protect him at school instills perfectly valid forms of faith suited to this stage in his life.

family

(FAM-uh-lee)

noun

People living together as a household who may be related by birth, marriage, or adoption.

Our FAMILY has grown over the years, and we now have a baby sister and an older stepbrother.

There are few words that have shifted in meaning as much as the word "family." A family used to typically mean two parents, children, and perhaps a beloved dog. Today families come in all shapes and sizes and there is no one way to describe a typical family. Children have no preconceived notion of what makes a "traditional" family. They simply consider their family to be those they love and coexist with, whether this is just mom and dad, a sibling, siblings brought in through another marriage, or just themselves with one parent. Whatever the make-up of your family, these are the people your children grow up with, create memories with, and depend on. It's your child's family that keeps her supported throughout every phase of her life.

fear

(feer)

noun

A feeling of anxiety related to something that scares you.

I didn't want to let my FEAR of the water keep me from learning to swim.

Being scared is part of being a kid, and children's fears, both rational and irrational, come and go as quickly as their interest in a toy. Adults know that while some fear is healthy, too much of it can produce a distracting anxiety, and can even keep a child from enjoying everyday activities. Let your child know that fear is normal, and that even adults are afraid from time to time. Sharing a fear that you had when you were young—perhaps a fear of the dark, or maybe spiders—will help your child understand that certain things just aren't as scary as they seem.

flexible

(FLECK-suh-bull)

adjective

Being able to adapt or make changes as a situation calls for it.

I wanted to be FLEXIBLE, so I agreed to see the movie that everyone else was interested in.

It's not always fun to be the person who has to be flexible, and it can be frustrating to change your plans based on the needs of someone else. However, adults understand that being a well-adjusted person means occasionally being flexible. As you adjust your life to accommodate the many needs of your children, remember that they will soon be put in the position of having to adjust to life's ups and downs. Let them know that they will have to be flexible in various situations. It's simply not possible to have everything in life go the way your child wants it to go. Teaching your child to be flexible will prepare him properly for what life throws at him—whether it be changes at school or at home. While it can be difficult for a child to be flexible, also be sure that he knows that there are times when others will reciprocate to accommodate his needs.

forgive

(fore-GIHV)

verb

To excuse a fault or a mistake caused by someone else.

When I FORGIVE someone, I immediately feel comforted by the sense of peace that accompanies such an action.

As adults, we've been in many situations that require us to forgive someone or to ask for forgiveness. Learning to forgive hurt feelings, offenses best forgotten, and others' mistakes is essential to leading a healthy, well-adjusted life. Children can learn to forgive very early on by being gracious with friends who say something out of turn or with parents who occasionally forget what's important. By teaching your children to forgive now, they'll learn that letting go is much more important than wasting their energy by holding on to unnecessary anger.

friendship

(FREND-ship)

noun

A relationship between people who share mutual trust and who provide support to one another.

My FRIENDSHIP with Stephen, whom I met when I was four, has lasted for many years.

Adults know that friendships come and go and that we are lucky if we have a few close friends in our lives. Our circumstances, interests, and needs all affect what kinds of friendships we maintain over the years. Children are likely to experience many friendships as they grow up, and not all of them will last. But while it's perfectly normal for children to drift apart from other kids, it's still important for them to develop an understanding of the true meaning of friendship. Let them know that a good friend is there for you, can be trusted, and is, of course, fun to be with.

frustration

(fruh-STRAY-shun)

noun

The feeling of disappointment, anger, or exhaustion that comes from facing a challenge.

I tried hard to finish the project, but my FRUSTRATION made it difficult.

Parents are no strangers to frustration, as convincing a child to do something he doesn't want to do often involves a tremendous challenge. This is normal, but finding ways to cope with frustration makes each day easier. Children experience frustration when they can't have what they want or can't complete a task effortlessly. Explain to your child that parents feel frustration, too—but by remaining calm and taking a step back, we can often see that our frustration isn't worth the energy, making it easier for us to manage whatever we find challenging.

future

(FYOO-chur)

noun

The period of time that hasn't arrived yet.

Even though the FUTURE is far off, I spend plenty of time imagining what it will be like.

Every parent has ideas about what his or her children's future will hold. Will they follow in your footsteps? Go to a good college? Become a writer, a lawyer, pursue medicine, be a parent? The future is a difficult concept for a child to grasp. Children have trouble waiting to do an activity that's just a few days away, so their adulthood is likely to seem so far away as to be irrelevant. You can start to give your child an understanding of this concept by talking about the future as being the period when they are a "big kid," a "teenager," and eventually a grownup. They'll see that all of those milestones are far away from their current existence but still remain relevant.

gentle

(JEN-tull)

adjective

Mild or kind in disposition or treatment.

I always need to remember to be GENTLE with my baby sister.

Most children will happily agree to be gentle when holding a younger sibling, playing with a new puppy, or being allowed to hold a delicate object. It's also important to teach your child that gentleness is also a wonderful part of many people's personalities. Not everyone likes to play roughly and loudly. Some children are naturally quiet and reserved, and these qualities should be respected. Even if your child is not gentle by nature overall, encourage him to appreciate and take note of the gentler side of his personality.

genuine

(JEN-yoo-in)

adjective

Being honest and open in relationships with others.

My mom is a very GENUINE person. She would never say she likes something if she doesn't.

When you have a genuine friend, you can trust him to give you the best advice, be there for you, and even tell you when you are about to make a mistake. Children don't like to hear that they are going about something the wrong way—even from another child. Tell your children that their genuine loved ones, the people who know them best, are often more skilled than they are at knowing when they are headed down the wrong path. Make sure your child understands that a genuine person is someone she knows well and who always has her best interests at heart.

give

(gihv)

verb

To bestow something of value on another person—a material object, your time, advice, or information.

My entire family makes it a point to GIVE something special to charity every holiday season.

All parents want their children to feel secure and it's also natural for parents to want their children to believe that every person in the world gets what they need. It is important that children understand that they have the power to give to others—ultimately improving their lives. Talk to your children about how you have been positively impacted when someone gave you an opportunity, their time, or their expertise. Discuss how they might give to others: Can they give their time? Are they willing to donate toys? The act of giving to another person will make your child feel happy and accomplished.

goal

(gole)

noun

A desired purpose or outcome.

My GOAL for this year is to learn to speak French.

While adults are used to setting and reaching goals, children tend to expect immediate results, which can make setting long-term goals difficult. Teaching your children to be proud of the milestones they reach can help lay the foundation for future goal setting. Celebrate the first time they finish an art project on their own, learn a new word, or write their names. While learning the alphabet and numbers is part of growing up, mastering these tasks is basically a way of reaching some important goals. Tell your children about goals you have set in your life and how it felt when you reached them.

gossip

(GOSS-up)

noun

Personal information pertaining to other people that is spread around, often with unkind intent.

I try very hard not to listen to the GOSSIP in the cafeteria.

Everyone is guilty of participating in the occasional round of gossip, and it's natural to want to know what people are talking about, especially when it involves personal information about a neighbor or acquaintance. Unfortunately, text messaging and social media have made it easier than ever for kids to gossip, which often results in misunderstandings and hurt feelings. Teach your children that gossip is hurtful and should be avoided. Encourage them to stand up to those who insist on spreading malicious and inaccurate information.

graciousness

(GRAY-shuss-niss)

noun

Polite behavior characterized by the ability to both tolerate and forgive others.

Warmly welcoming the extra guests at our dinner party is another example of my mother's GRACIOUSNESS.

Graciousness can be a difficult quality to cultivate. Life is hard enough without having to make additional and sometimes unexpected accommodations—it's often easier to just say no. But if you think about times you've chosen to be gracious, it's likely that you'll find that your willingness to be open and inviting resulted in a positive experience. Tell your children that being sociable and flexible when unexpected events pop up can actually result in even more fun for everyone. The more occasions your children have to be gracious, the more naturally it will come, and the easier it will be for them to manage the unexpected.

gratitude

(GRAT-ih-tood)

noun

Thankfulness to someone for having helped you.

I try to show my GRATITUDE to my mom for all she does as often as I can.

It's easy for parents to feel that everything they do goes unappreciated. Caring for children is incredibly difficult, and unfortunately kids don't realize how much energy it takes to shop, clean, prepare meals, do laundry, and keep them entertained. Start to teach your children about gratitude by simply encouraging them to say thank you when you make them lunch or take them to the park. Soon gratitude will be something that's ingrained in your children and they'll start to understand the effort it takes for other people to help them out.

health

(hellth)

noun

The condition of your mind and body.

We exercise and eat fruits and vegetables to make sure we maintain good HEALTH.

All parents want good health for their children, but getting your child to exercise and eat healthful foods is often easier said than done. Commit to providing an example of good health for your children. Aim for daily exercise for both you and your children and introduce healthy foods into your family's diet. Teach your children that a large part of being healthy is taking care of their mind and spirit and that they should get plenty of sleep and live their lives to the fullest. Enjoy playing with your children, and be sure to cultivate relationships and hobbies that enhance your—and their—overall state of well-being.

help

(hellp)

verb

To provide someone with something they need, such as advice, physical assistance, or information.

After struggling with the math problem for half an hour, I realized that I needed someone to HELP me.

Everyone, at one time or another, needs help. Unfortunately, in today's busy society, adults may worry that others are simply too busy to take the time to lend a hand and are often reluctant to ask for help. Teach your child that needing help is natural, and it isn't something that she should be reluctant to ask for. There is no shame in needing assistance, and the bottom line is that life would be easier for everyone if they were simply comfortable accepting help from a well-meaning neighbor or friend from time to time. In addition, children are generally afraid to ask for help because they are used to parents coming to the rescue when they can't reach something, are hungry, scared, or just can't figure something out. Take cues from your child—don't be afraid to ask for help. It's likely that you'll find a friend or neighbor who is more than willing to be of service . . . and you can be sure to let him or her know that you're there to return the favor.

hero

(HERE-oh)

noun

A person who commits admirable acts, or has a unique strength of character that inspires others.

My third-grade teacher, who helped me learn to read, is a personal HERO of mine.

It would be so easy for a child to equate the word "hero" with Spider-Man, Batman, or one of the other superheroes that are so prevalent in popular culture, but it's important for kids to understand that being a hero is more about courage and conviction than physical strength. Having a true hero to look up to can be a wonderful experience for a child as a hero can provide your child with a strong example of how to behave and how to treat others. Tell them about the heroes you've encountered in your life—such as a special teacher, an activist, or a family member—and explain why they mean so much to you.

history

(HISS-tuh-ree)

noun

The events of the past, in the lives of individual persons, in families, or in societies.

The town I live in has a unique and vibrant HISTORY.

History is a huge concept and limiting your child's understanding of history to what he learns in school might not accurately convey its importance. While it's important to understand and appreciate the events that have happened in national and world history, it's also nice to have an understanding of the history of your own family. Teaching your children about the lives of their grandparents, greatgrandparents, and other distant relatives not only can inspire a love of learning about the past, but can create a deeper sense of closeness within your family.

home

(home)

noun

The physical place where a person lives his life, often with family or friends.

Peter was so happy to enjoy the comforts of HOME after being away at camp.

Many childhood memories take place in the home, which is why it's so important that your home is a comfortable, loving, and stimulating environment. Home is where your children take their first steps, celebrate holidays, share meals, do their homework or study, and play with friends. Home is also the most sought-out place of solace when they are feeling tired, sad, or stressed. By placing importance on your home—by decorating it, spending family time together in it, and opening it up to others for special occasions—you'll teach your children that home is a special place that will always be there for them.

humility

(hyoo-MILL-uh-tee)

noun

The quality of being respectful or unassuming.

Everyone thought Mary was incredibly pretty and talented, but her HUMILITY kept her from becoming arrogant.

Since most parents can't help but shower their children with praise and love, humility can be a hard concept for a child to grasp. While there's no reason to stop piling the compliments on your children, it's a good idea to teach them how to handle compliments from others. Explain to them that they should be gracious when receiving praise. It's okay to take a compliment to heart, and to feel proud, but that doesn't mean that they can allow themselves to believe they are better than anyone else. Children should learn to say "thank you" and strive to behave in a manner that warrants further praise.

humor

(HEW-mur)

noun

The element that makes something funny.

We all got soaking wet at the baseball game, but luckily everyone could appreciate the HUMOR of the situation.

It isn't always easy to understand our children's sense of humor, but by trying to jump in and laugh with them, you'll set the foundation for a quality that serves everyone well in life. Also remember to occasionally laugh when you'd rather scream. Laughing rather than scolding when your child accidentally sprays you with the garden hose or spills milk on your favorite sweater teaches her that our minor discomforts are no big deal . . . sometimes you can just laugh them off. If your children become accustomed to you having a sense of humor when life becomes complicated, they'll learn that it's sometimes better to simply laugh something off than become frustrated or angry.

imagination

(ih-maj-uh-NAY-shun)

noun

The ability to form ideas, pictures, or concepts in your mind to create something new or solve a challenging problem.

I use my IMAGINATION to think about playing on a sunny beach when it's raining outside.

The ability to use imagination to improve our lives is a great gift. It's easy to forget that our imagination is not just a way to make our world more creative and unique, but that it can also be used to make life a bit easier. We face problems and challenges every day—and our imagination is there to help. Children instinctively use their imagination in everything they do, from playing with friends to figuring out how to get Mom to buy that new toy they desperately want. Show your child how using her imagination can be beneficial. Imagination is more than daydreaming and your child can use her imagination to come up with new ideas, and even to figure out how to solve problems.

improvise

(IMM-pruh-vize)

verb

To make do out of necessity with what's presently available to you.

It rained on the day of our picnic, forcing us to IMPROVISE new plans.

Adults know that life doesn't always go as smoothly as we hope it will and are accustomed to quick last-minute changes. You are able to make do with different materials when working on a project, know how to substitute ingredients when cooking, and can adjust plans whenever necessary. Children, on the other hand, can easily become frustrated when things don't go as planned, and even if an equally good solution is presented, they may be reluctant to accept it. Show your child that improvisation can be fun, and that unexpected surprises may come their way when they remain open to a change of plans.

independence

(in-dee-PEN-dens)

noun

The quality of not being dependent on other people or other outside forces.

In order to increase my INDEPENDENCE, I now choose my own clothes and get dressed by myself.

It's easy for parents to think their children will never be independent. Children depend on parents for so much—everything from meals to getting dressed and bathing to creating a fun and stimulating schedule of activities. It's important to remember that children need some independence to develop and grow, so spend some time thinking about how your children can benefit from some independence. If your child is an early riser, try having him wake up on his own. If your child likes to help in the kitchen, put him in charge of setting or clearing the table. These simple tasks will increase your child's confidence and ultimately make your job easier.

insightful

(in-SITE-full)

adjective

Possessing the ability to notice small details about a person or situation.

The fact that my teacher could tell that I was sad showed how INSIGHTFUL she was.

Children have a natural ability to know when someone is upset, anxious, or sad, and tend to be even more insightful than adults. Kids aren't afraid to ask if someone is having a bad day, or is unhappy about something. They instinctively know that people's feelings need to be validated. Show your child how taking the time to ask when a friend or family member seems troubled is sometimes the simplest way to make someone feel better. If children see firsthand that being insightful positively affects their relationships, they'll continue to develop this quality and use it throughout their lives.

inspiration

(in-spuh-RAY-shun)

noun

A quality that encourages you to create something or have a new perspective.

The flowers in our garden were my INSPIRATION for the painting.

Children can find inspiration anywhere—in nature, stories, their friends, and even their toys—so encourage your children to play, create, and be inspired. Build a fort with them and let them pretend they are pirates. Take them to the zoo with a sketchpad and pencils and see what kinds of creations they come up with. Give them access to different materials— pencils, crayons, markers, tape, string, old magazines, boxes, etc.—and enjoy the designs they make.

integrity

(in-TEG-rih-tee)

noun

High professional or personal standards.

My sense of INTEGRITY kept me from accepting praise for something I didn't do.

Integrity can be a difficult quality to maintain. Sometimes we feel pressured to compromise. While it's important for children to know that compromise can be essential, they should know that it's okay to step away when something goes against their sense of integrity. Children develop a sense of what's right and wrong at a young age, with the help of their parents. As they continue to develop their sense of right and wrong, teach them what to do in situations when they're encouraged to compromise their integrity. Talk about how they'll respond when they are put in a position to do something that they feel is wrong.

intelligence

(in-TELL-uh-jens)

noun

The ability to absorb and use knowledge.

My brother's INTELLIGENCE made it easy for him to excel in math and science.

There are many traits that are valued in a child. You want your children to be kind to others and sweet to your family. You hope they will be happy and have a sense of humor. And you also hope that they'll be intelligent, an important quality that children should be taught to appreciate and recognize. Teaching your children that intelligence is a highly desirable quality—and that it should be cultivated in themselves and admired in others—will help ensure that they develop a sense of what matters most in people.

joy

(joi)

noun

A feeling of great happiness brought on by something exciting or pleasurable.

I feel so much JOY when I wake up on Christmas morning.

Children are experts at feeling joy. A visit to the zoo, an ice cream cone, or even a play date with a friend are all likely to bring out that feeling in your child. Adults often wish that they could feel joy as easily as children do, so increase the joy in your life by taking pleasure in the happiness that your child experiences. Enjoy the moment when you tell your child you're coming home early to take her to the park, or find joy in the expression on your child's face when you tell her she can stay up late with you to watch an extra cartoon. Be sure to tell your child that her ability to feel and create joy in those around her is a treasured quality. Joy is infectious, and she should be proud of her ability to spread the feeling to others.

justice

(JUSS-tiss)

noun

Fairness and reasonableness in making decisions or interacting with other people.

We had to remember to use our sense of JUSTICE while making a choice about who would be the class leader.

Justice might be one of the most difficult concepts to explain to a child. As you know, while all children want to be treated fairly, it's not always easy to get them to reciprocate. Children want what they want when they want it, and in such circumstances any sense of justice is going to go out the window. When making choices involving your children, point out how you make a conscious decision to be fair. For example, today it's your older child's turn to choose a TV show, because your younger child did it last time. Eventually they will learn that justice is a concept that can benefit everyone.

kindness

(KYNDE-niss)

noun

Consideration and good will toward another person.

My mom had a really bad day at work, so we were sure to shower her with as much KINDNESS as possible.

Kindness is one of the best traits a person can possess. When you think about the people you are drawn to in life, it's typically the people who are kind and giving who often stick out. Luckily, there are so many little ways for a child to show kindness toward a family member, friend, or teacher that it's relatively easy to teach children to be kind. Simply show them that drawing a nice picture for someone or taking the time to ask people how they are feeling are the simple types of gestures that are associated with kindness.

knowledge

(NOLL-idj)

noun

A clear awareness of a situation; information possessed about a particular topic.

My KNOWLEDGE of dinosaurs grows and I strive to learn more.

Your expertise might fall in the category of cooking, car repair, or photography, but everyone is knowledgeable about a particular area. Children tend to associate the concept of knowledge with school, with working hard in class and doing homework, so explain how and why you possess the knowledge that you do. Make sure your child understands that he can be knowledgeable about any area he chooses and that he's passionate about. He may become an expert on dinosaurs, baseball players, or chemistry, and that's great!

laughter

(LAFF-tur)

noun

A sound expressing happiness and amusement.

Our LAUGHTER was so loud it could be heard all the way down the street.

Laughter is sometimes so common that we take it for granted. You probably find yourself laughing about something every day. It's also true that most parents find great joy in the sound of their child's laughter. Make a point to laugh with your children about whatever they find amusing: a cartoon, a make-believe game, or something silly you've done. Laughing is one of the best ways you can bond with your children, so make it a point to fully appreciate the funny moments you share with your kids. They'll appreciate it too!

limitation

(lih-mih-TAY-shun)

noun

A restriction that is difficult for a person to overcome.

I have difficulties reading. This LIMITATION means I have to take my time and be patient with myself.

We all have limitations; some are easier to overcome than others. It's often painful for parents to watch their child struggle —whether it be with a tough subject, with their feelings, or even with a physical handicap. Children often feel alone when it comes to their limitations, and it's easy for them to believe that they are the only one who has trouble reading or making friends. Convince your children that everyone has limitations by being open about your own. Let them know that even though you are older and wiser you are still plagued by limitations, but have managed to succeed in spite of them.

listen

(LISS-in)

verb

To pay close attention to what someone is saying.

If I LISTEN carefully to my friends, I can learn more about what they like and want.

Most parents have said "my kid never listens" on many occasions. It's incredibly frustrating to feel that your questions and requests go unheard. Parents also know that young children sometimes communicate their needs in a way that only an attentive mother or father can understand. Explain to your child that you make a point not only to listen but to understand what they need. Also tell them that by listening carefully to others, they'll be able to be a better friend or family member. A person who truly listens and understands the needs of others is special and rare, and is greatly valued by other people.

literature

(LITT-ur-uh-chur)

noun

Written works of fiction, poetry, criticism, and journalism of excellent quality that have a lasting value.

I look forward to being able to enjoy the great works of LITERATURE when I get a little older.

Reading to your child is one of the greatest joys of being a parent, and it's delightful to watch your child develop favorite stories and characters. It's never too early to start talking to your child about what makes a particular book great. While it may be a long time before she can handle the works of Jane Austen or Tolstoy, it's perfectly acceptable to talk about the value of Harry Potter and Eloise. Showing your appreciation for vibrant characters and compelling stories will help your children develop their love of literature and will encourage them to explore books on their own as they grow older.

loneliness

(LONE-lee-niss)

noun

A feeling of sadness because you are alone or isolated.

I experienced a great sense of LONELINESS when my friends went to the movies without me.

Everyone experiences loneliness at times, but most parents spend so much time surrounded by family that they eventually learn to cherish any time they get to themselves. However, it is inevitable that your child will experience loneliness on occasion. Sometimes he'll feel left out at school, or maybe he'll feel frustrated when an older sibling won't let him join in the fun. Let your child know that everyone experiences loneliness at some time. However, being lonely doesn't have to mean being sad or bored. Encourage your child to entertain himself at these times. Explain how reading a book, getting lost in a favorite movie, or enjoying an art project are fantastic ways to keep loneliness at bay.

loss

(lawss)

noun

The disappearance of a beloved person or object from your life, or a serious disappointment.

The LOSS of my favorite teddy bear made it difficult for me to sleep.

All parents pray that their children will never have to suffer through a horrible loss. As much as you would like to prevent it, however, your children will likely experience some sort of loss before they become adults. Whether your children have to deal with the loss of a family pet or a grandparent, help them to understand that any feelings of sadness, anger, or confusion are completely appropriate, and be sure to share any feelings that you're having. Let your children know that, while this is an incredibly sad time, families get through loss together and eventually manage to feel better.

love

(luhv)

noun

Great feelings of happiness and affection elicited by a person or thing.

I am always grateful for the LOVE I feel for my family and friends.

It's wonderful for parents to see how children have an innate understanding of the concept of love. In fact, hearing "I love you" from your child is one of the greatest pleasures of being a parent. You want your children to know that you love them, and you do this by caring for them and showing them affection. Help your child develop her sense of love by being open about your own various passions. Show her how, in addition to loving your family and friends, you also love art, music, literature, sports, or cooking. Sharing a mutual love of various ideas or activities is a great way to become closer to your child.

loyalty

(LOI-ul-tee)

noun

Faithfulness to a decision, person, or idea.

Your LOYALTY toward our school helps to make it a better place.

Children can change their minds about their feelings toward anything—a friend, sibling, teacher, game, or toy—within seconds, but adults know that the rash decisions children make often don't reflect their true feelings about a situation. The good news is that exposing them to the concept of loyalty might make them think twice about making strong decisions when it comes to people. Teach your child that, while it's okay for him to change his mind, it's his loyalty that connects him to other people and sets the foundation for strong friendships.

luck

(luhk)

noun

The possession of good fortune sometimes experienced by chance.

It was LUCK that helped us find our kitten when he was lost.

Who doesn't wish for a little bit of luck now and then? It's easy to think that luck, rather than your own actions, is responsible for the good things that happen to you or to other people, and, in fact, everyone experiences positive things that happen due to forces that are outside of their control. Let your child know that it's possible for him to make his own luck. If he wants something, how can he go about getting it? Hard work? Practice? Saving money? Meeting new people? All of these elements will help your child increase his chances of luck finding him. The sooner he understands that luck, to some extent, is within his control, the more empowered he'll feel.

manners

(MAN-urs)

noun

Social behaviors that are considered appropriate.

I must remember to use my MANNERS and say "please" and "thank you" when it is suitable to do so.

At times it might seem that it's impossible to teach your kids how to behave. Kids are loud, fast, and impatient, and it's not particularly easy to get them to settle down. The idea of taking them to a restaurant or to someone else's house can be overwhelming. Remember that by following your example, your child will learn manners. Remind yourself that your child may actually be exhibiting age-appropriate behavior and it's not an indication that she has no manners. Encourage her "pleases," "thank yous," and "your welcomes." She'll be well on her way to being the polite and mindful child you're hoping to have.

maturity

(muh-CHOOR-uh-tee)

noun

A state of being fully aged or grown, especially mentally and emotionally.

My MATURITY kept me from laughing when my sister fell off the slide.

No parent wants a child to grow up too quickly. You likely relish the time you have with your children, and it can be hard to accept that they will eventually rely on you less and less. To help your child transition to the next stage in life, be sure to instill a strong sense of maturity. Talk to your child about how he feels about important issues, how he would make certain decisions, and what his hopes and dreams are and how he plans to execute them. Such conversations will give you a good sense of whether or not your child is ready to make his way in the world on his own.

memory

(MEM-uh-ree)

noun

An experience recalled from your past.

Enjoying a bright red popsicle on a warm afternoon brings a sweet MEMORY of summer.

Children are constantly creating memories, even on an ordinary day. In fact, it's often the little things—the meals you share, the books you read, and the trips you take to the park—that lay the groundwork for a childhood full of wonderful memories. And the event doesn't need to be extravagant to produce the foundation of a good memory. Children are just as likely to enjoy a memory of cooking together or making special art projects as they are an elaborate family vacation. Simply spending quality time with your child and appreciating every moment will result in good memories for both of you.

mentor

(MEN-tore)

noun

An experienced person in your life who helps you by providing advice and support and encourages your personal growth.

I was lucky to find a MENTOR who was willing to help me improve my understanding of science.

Everyone has valuable skills and experience that can be shared, and the world would be a better place if more people took the time to mentor someone else. Perhaps you had a mentor who helped you with your career, or who provided parenting advice when you needed it most. When your child shows an interest in a particular area, consider finding her a mentor from your circle of friends and colleagues. Mentorship can shape the direction of a young person's life and help her get her foot in the door job-wise when the time comes. If your child is showing an interest in the sciences, a particular sport, or the arts, the right mentor can make the difference between your child developing a lifelong passion versus a passing interest.

mindfulness

(MIND-full-niss)

noun

A strong presence of mind; the act of making a point to pay attention to the present.

By practicing MINDFULNESS, you can be sure to remember how many blessings you have in life.

Life has never been more distracting. Today's parents are torn in hundreds of different directions, which can make it difficult for them to focus on the positive aspects of their lives. Since children take their cues from you, it's possible that they too will have trouble focusing on the good. They might start to think about what they feel they don't have—enough time with their parents, enough toys, the right clothes, etc. Tell your child how important it is to live in the present. Let him know that you make a point to practice mindfulness, allowing you to appreciate how much you love your family, home, and friends.

miracle

(MEER-uh-kull)

noun

An unexpected event or action that seemed extremely unlikely to occur.

After all the rain, it felt like a MIRACLE when the sun came out the minute the game was supposed to begin.

It's easy to associate miracles with otherworldly ideas, and, when initially asked about miracles, it's likely that most adults would say that they haven't experienced a true miracle. But for children, miracles occur frequently. Each change in season, each unforeseen happy ending, and every beautiful day feels like a miracle for them. Learn from what your child finds to marvel at in her world. Spend some time thinking about amazing things you have experienced—the birth of your children, your wedding day, or watching your child's first steps—and make sure to share experiences like these with your child. By making sure that your child understands that miracles do actually occur in everyday life, you will help her develop an appreciation of all the little things that make the world an amazing place in which to live.

mischief

(MISS-chiff)

noun

Behavior that is considered undesirable, but not with mean intent.

My dad and I love MISCHIEF—we especially enjoy playing an occasional joke on my mom.

Parents know that there is a big difference between harmless mischief and truly bad behavior. While your child playing a joke on you or behaving in a way that's slightly inappropriate can be annoying, remember that it's part of being a kid, and he is enjoying his antics. Try to appreciate the mischievous side of your child. Just make sure that he understands that there is a time and place for such behavior—at home might be fine, but not at school or at a friend's house.

mission

(MISH-un)

noun

A specific duty or task that a person believes he or she should carry out.

I'm making it my MISSION in life to encourage people to be kind to animals.

It may be a bit much to expect your child to have a mission. It often takes adults years to figure out what their mission is, and it's not unusual to find an adult who's still searching. A mission involves dedication, focus, and drive. Tell your child how you value those who have embarked successfully on a mission. If you've had a mission in your life—whether it be raising a happy family or fighting for a cause you believe in— tell your child why it's been important to you and how you've gone about accomplishing your mission. By sharing your path with your child, you'll show her that all desires in life take work and dedication. More importantly, she'll see that all of this work is completely worth the extra effort.

mistake

(mih-STAKE)

noun

An unwise decision often caused by poor judgment.

It was a MISTAKE to think that I could wait until the night before to study for my history test and still do well.

Making mistakes is a big part of being a child, and while it's incredibly difficult to watch your children struggle and deal with the consequences when they make a bad choice, it's crucial to their development that they be allowed to do so. While you obviously wouldn't allow your child to make a mistake that would result in her being unsafe, it is important to let her experience the results that a bad choice can bring. As painful as it may be to do, children must be allowed to make choices—and when they neglect to make a good one, they will learn from the result of their actions.

modest

(MAHD-ist)

adjective

Not drawing attention to your skills, achievements, or talents.

I try to be MODEST about the fact that I'm the fastest runner on the playground.

Parents want their children to be proud of their accomplishments and abilities. You likely praise them when they do well, so they know that they're improving and can feel good about themselves. But what do you do when they start to become a little too proud? No one wants his child to brag or appear conceited. Explain to your child that while it's perfectly acceptable for her to feel proud of her achievements or talents, it's not okay to be immodest. Bragging about an ability just makes others feel bad.

moral

(MORE-ul)

adjective

Conforming to standards of right or good according to your conscience.

It isn't MORAL to lie, cheat, or steal.

Parents are always helping their children determine what is right and wrong. You want your children to be able to share, act kindly toward friends, and understand that lying, cheating, and stealing are wrong. Obviously, as they get older you also want them to have an understanding of greater moral issues like war, crime, and discrimination. Until they are ready to deal with larger concepts, make a point of explaining why you feel that a particular action they've chosen to take is or isn't moral. For instance, let them know that one lie often just leads to more, but also that a positive action leads to good feelings. Make it clear to your children that you expect that the path they choose to take in life will be a moral one.

motivation

(moe-tuh-VAY-shun)

noun

The incentive to remain engaged in a pursuit or activity.

I was really losing my MOTIVATION, so my mom reminded me that we would celebrate when I finished my school project.

Adults know how hard it is to stay motivated and how easily frustrations, obstacles, and random difficulties can throw you off course. Children, with their shortened attention spans, can lose motivation at the drop of a hat. Remember that it's normal for your child to lose interest in finishing a project or playing a musical instrument. Make a point of keeping your child's motivation high and exposing him to whatever he needs to stay on track. Talk to him about what you do when you lose motivation. Before you know it, your child will be back at work and closer to accomplishing what he set out to do.

nature

(NAY-chur)

noun

Every part of the outside world, including the plants and animals that exist in our physical world.

I feel very calm and peaceful after spending a day out in NATURE.

If you were to describe your average day, it's likely the word "complicated" would come up. Parents have so many responsibilities and obligations today that it's almost impossible to finish everything that they need to do before it's time to go to bed. Your children will eventually notice if you become too stressed out and frazzled, so make a point of taking your children outside to enjoy the natural world where all of you can unwind. An afternoon spent in a local woods, by a lake, or even in a green city park can be incredibly refreshing. Your children will learn to appreciate the outdoors, which is a crucial part of a healthy, active lifestyle. They will soon realize that being outside, and getting away from electronics such as TVs, cell phones, and video games is actually an enjoyable way to spend their time.

neighborhood

(NAY-bur-hood)

noun

The local community in which you live.

My NEIGHBORHOOD looks so pretty after a snowfall.

People are so busy today that there isn't as much time for socializing as there used to be. Unfortunately, this can make it difficult to get to know the other people in your neighborhood. Make a point of getting to know your neighbors with your child and teach him to be courteous to those who live around you. Explain that what makes a neighborhood special are the unique characteristics that give it its own personality. It's also fun to make a point of getting to know shopkeepers and the people who own local restaurants. Your child will soon develop a sense that he is an important part of a larger community.

open

(OH-pun)

adjective

Not trying to hide anything; ready to accept new ideas and concepts.

I try to remain OPEN to any new and fun ideas that my friends have.

Most adults like to think of themselves as "open-minded," but are you truly open when faced with changes at home or at work? It can be challenging to break from your routine and try to incorporate someone else's ideas into your lifestyle, but by staying open, you put yourself in a position to be changed for the better by new ideas and concepts. Talk to your children about how you try to be as open to other people's ideas as possible. Encourage them to think about and try new things before simply deciding that they won't work.

opportunity

(opp-ur-TOO-nih-tee)

noun

A chance to have a unique experience or gain an advantage.

I was thrilled to have the OPPORTUNITY to travel to Washington, D.C., with my classmates.

Adults can see an opportunity long before a young person can. It's not unusual for children to be somewhat short-sighted, and only focus on the challenge of a particular situation instead of seeing the long-term benefit. Fears and anxiety can also make taking advantage of an opportunity challenging. For example, fears about leaving home and traveling can keep a child from seeing all the benefits of experiencing a new culture, new places, and new people. Show your child that opportunities are often accompanied by challenge, and that it's worth it to face your fears to have new and exciting experiences.

organize

(OR-geh-nyze)

verb

To carefully arrange a group of objects in a structured manner.

It's so much easier to get ready for school in the morning when I ORGANIZE my homework the night before.

If you were to step into a child's room, it's likely that "organized" wouldn't be one of the first words you would use to describe it. Children love to spread out and make a mess, but adults understand that spending some time organizing ultimately makes life easier. While you may not want to waste your efforts trying to get your kids to organize their toys, it is helpful to encourage them to be organized in other areas. Emphasize how keeping their clothes and schoolwork organized will mean that they'll have more time for playing, activities, and seeing friends.

participate

(parr-TISS-uh-payte)

verb

To take part in a specific event or activity.

I was glad that I decided to PARTICIPATE in the fundraiser at school—it was lots of fun.

Over the course of your life, you've likely been in many situations that you haven't wanted to be in. Maybe there was a school event, work function, or neighborhood party that you just didn't want to go to. However, it's not unusual to find that once you choose to participate in such an event, you end up having a great time and aren't sure why you were reluctant to go in the first place. Children have a tendency to get set in their ways, and trying something new—or being pulled away from an intense session of coloring or train building—can be frustrating. If you encourage your children to participate in new things, it's likely that they too will enjoy the new activity more than they thought they would. Let them know that you are often reluctant to join in, but you are always glad that you ultimately chose to participate.

passion

(PASH-un)

noun

A strong love for an activity or hobby.

I enjoy many activities, but baseball is my true PASSION.

Adults know that there are many forms of passion, but for a child, passion generally arrives in the form of love for a particular hobby, sport, game, or activity. While you can't predict or determine what your child's passion will ultimately be, you can find great joy in watching a passion grow. Exposing your child to many different activities and letting him determine what feels right for him can help him discover a passion early on. Your child might fall in love with piano, baseball, soccer, or ballet. Once he finds that passion, enjoy watching him excel and grow.

patience

(PAY-shens)

noun

The ability to wait without becoming angry or upset, or to remain calm and collected when faced with a challenge.

Waiting to blow out the candles while everyone sang "Happy Birthday" took lots of PATIENCE.

Patience is difficult, especially for kids. Why wait when you can cry, have a tantrum, or just beg until someone gets you what you want? Teach your children to be patient to the best of their ability early on. Life requires an immense amount of patience, whether you're waiting for someone to decide if you're the right person for the job, or you're in line with a crowd at an amusement park. Through your example, children will eventually understand that what they're seeking out is usually worth the wait.

peace

(peece)

noun

A sense of calm; an end to hostilities between people who are at odds with each other.

PEACE was restored in our house after my sister and mom stopped arguing.

While it's important for children to eventually understand the larger concept of peace—and how the world would be a better place without war, hostility, and fighting—peace in the home is important, too. Arguments, even minor disagreements, can disrupt the peaceful environment you've likely worked hard to create. Let your child know that you expect and appreciate a sense of calm at home, and that her behavior has a direct impact on whether or not that happens.

persevere

(pur-suh-VEER)

verb

To hold on to a belief or continue with an activity after encountering problems, even over a long period of time.

If we wanted to continue with our camping trip, we had to PERSEVERE despite the bad weather.

Children's lives tend to be defined by fast-paced games and activities—kids are accustomed to things happening quickly. Because of this, it's natural for a child to want to change gears when he encounters a problem, rather than work to find a solution. As an adult you know that much would be missed out on if you let every obstacle stop you from doing what you want, so show your children how perseverance can mean the difference between having a wonderful experience and experiencing nothing at all. Encourage them to find solutions to their problems and watch them enjoy the reward.

playful

(PLAY-full)

adjective

Able to enjoy yourself, play games, and tease in a kind fashion.

It makes me so happy when my father is in a PLAYFUL mood on weekends.

It takes so much effort to keep a family on track that you could easily spend the majority of your time doing laundry, shopping, cooking, paying bills, and picking up after kids. Unfortunately, this go-getting lifestyle can make it difficult to actually find time to play with your kids and show them how important it is to give yourself a break and relax. Give yourself permission to take a break and enjoy some quality time with your children. Have game night, play catch, do a craft, be silly. Your children will appreciate your playfulness, and you'll likely feel energized by your time with them.

power

(POW-ur)

noun

The ability or skill to control or influence the actions of other people.

The speaker had such POWER that I wanted to join her cause immediately.

"Power" is a complicated word that can have very positive or negative connotations. How do you teach a child to appreciate power at its best and be wary of it when appropriate? Tell your child which qualities you feel are positive forms of power, like character, conviction, dedication, and talent. It is also wise to teach your children that when power comes in the form of brute strength, it is something to be careful of. Your children shouldn't feel swayed by a "powerful" person if that person doesn't hold the characteristics that your children value. Otherwise it's possible this person could be leading them down a less than savory path.

practical

(PRACK-tih-kul)

adjective

Capable of remaining levelheaded when dealing with a problem or difficulty.

The decision to ask an adult for help rather than keep struggling to find a solution was very PRACTICAL.

Now that you have a family, you are probably required to be more practical than you would like to be. While being practical isn't fun, it's often necessary. Children aren't practical by nature, and it takes some convincing for them to agree to choose a toy that will last rather than something silly that they will quickly tire of. While it's fine to indulge your child on occasion, you should feel comfortable putting your foot down from time to time. By learning to be practical, your children learn what it's like to live in the real world.

praise

(prayze)

verb

To approve or admire a person's achievements, ideas, or actions.

My mom is always sure to PRAISE me when I get a good grade on a test.

Unfortunately, as we get older, we often don't receive as much praise as we'd like. Praise in the workplace can be rare, and you may feel that no one appreciates anything you do around the house or with your kids. Let your kids enjoy the praise they receive when they are young. Be sure to comment on a job well done when they do as they're told, make an extra effort around the house, or get a good grade at school. By freely expressing your praise, you may find that your children will begin to respond in a similar fashion by appreciating how much you do for them.

prepare

(pree-PAIR)

verb

To get ready for a particular event or activity.

It took a lot of time to PREPARE for our family's upcoming camping trip.

Parents are constantly preparing for something: a birthday party, a holiday, a work presentation, or just the week ahead. You carefully plan meals and schedules, knowing that if you didn't do these things in advance, life would be more complicated. In contrast, children aren't accustomed to preparing much in advance. They tend to be impulsive, and do things as they feel moved to. Talk to your children about how preparation can be helpful. Explain how the morning routine would be easier if they chose their clothes the night before . . . or how they might have time for an extra bedtime story if they planned to get ready for bed just a bit earlier. Encouraging your children to participate in preparations for the day will teach them responsibility, and will make your life just a little bit easier.

pretend

(pree-TEND)

verb

To believe something that isn't true through play or imagination.

I love haunted houses during Halloween. It's so much fun to PRETEND that ghosts and monsters are real, even though they can sometimes seem scary.

One of the most magical parts of childhood involves pretending, and it's great to watch your children make believe that they are astronauts, princesses, or crocodiles. Pretending encourages imagination and creativity, and is an essential part of their development. While you should encourage your child to pretend, you may also want to point out that some of his fears may be based on imaginary beings. He doesn't need to worry about things under the bed or ghosts in the attic. The sooner your child understands the concept of pretending, the more easily he will be able to rid himself of certain fears as well as successfully entertain fun fantasies.

pride

(pryde)

noun

Respect for yourself and your actions; the good feeling that comes from reaching a goal or having a special experience.

My mom takes PRIDE in bringing out the best qualities in me.

You praise your child for doing well in school, for mastering new tasks, and for simply being a good person. While your kids undoubtedly know how proud you are of them, how do you teach them to take pride in their actions? Instill this value by showing them that the things they do are a direct reflection of how they'll be viewed by the world. Would they take pride in being seen as kind and interesting people? Do they want to be people who take the extra time to comfort a friend? Explain that their actions have a direct impact on the sense of pride they'll feel.

privacy

(PRY-vuh-see)

noun

Freedom from the attention of others.

The only place where I can have PRIVACY is in my own bedroom.

It's not uncommon for parents to feel that they have no privacy whatsoever, as children—especially very young ones—follow their parents everywhere. By teaching your child that everyone needs privacy, you'll be showing her how to set up important standards in her life—and hopefully you'll get some privacy of your own as a result. Privacy is a particularly difficult concept to grasp today, as Facebook and Twitter can make much of our lives public so easily. Make sure your child understands the consequences of sharing too much personal information online. Help her see that when she posts private information online, she is potentially jeopardizing the privacy of herself, her family, and her friends.

privilege

(PRIV-uh-lihj)

noun

An advantage that isn't given to everybody else.

It was a real PRIVILEGE to go backstage after the performance.

Parents want to do special things for their children; you likely want your child to enjoy advantages and have opportunities that you didn't. While it's wonderful to introduce your child to places, people, and situations that will open doors and make life more interesting for him, it's also okay to let him know that this is a privilege. Talk to your child about a special event or activity. Let him know that there's a reason you're allowing him to participate, and that he needs to appreciate that what's happening is a special privilege. By sharing this information with your child, you'll show him that an activity is special, while also ensuring that he has appreciation for the opportunities he's given.

progress

(PROG-ress)

noun

A gradual forward motion as a person improves at something.

I was definitely making PROGRESS in my English class at school.

Adults are accustomed to being goal driven and it's not unusual for an adult to wait until a final goal is reached to take the time to pat himself on the back. For a child, reaching a goal can be a long process, so make sure your child stays motivated and on track by taking the time to acknowledge the progress she makes. No one goes from struggling with math to completely grasping the concepts overnight. Make sure your child knows that progress is part of the process, and you are proud of every step forward she makes.

question

(KWESS-chun)

noun

A feeling of doubt or uncertainty; an inquiry about an issue that needs to be examined or explained.

I felt better after my mom answered my QUESTION about my new school.

Children have endless questions and there is typically no end to their curiosity about a variety of subjects. While children are generally comfortable asking questions, make sure that they understand that it's crucial to ask questions when they are feeling doubt or uncertainty. It's okay to have doubts when something inside tells them that a situation isn't right. Tell them that they should come to you in such situations, and that you'll work together to figure out the correct course of action.

reality

(ree-AL-ih-tee)

noun

What actually exists, or could exist in real life.

The REALITY is, we'll have a lot of work to do after we move into our new house.

It's ironic that with all of the reality shows that are on television, it's more complicated than ever to instill a sense of what reality is in a child. Adults know that what's on reality television actually has little to do with the real world; few people are as wealthy, conceited, and complicated as the ones who are on such shows. Ground your child in reality by letting him know that most people work hard, spend time with their families, go to school, and enjoy time with their friends. It's not normal to fly off to an elaborate locale on a moment's notice, or have birthday parties for 200-plus people. While it's good to encourage your child to stretch and dream, don't let him think that his reality is any less wonderful than what he might see on TV.

regret

(ree-GREHT)

verb

To feel sorry or upset about a mistake you made or a hurtful action you inflicted upon another.

I REGRET not sharing my toys with my friend during our last play date.

Feeling regret is unpleasant, and everyone, at some point, regrets certain actions taken toward another person, things said, and opportunities not taken. While children may not immediately understand feelings of regret, they do know that they often feel badly after they misbehave or hurt another child. Explain to your child that regret can be avoided by taking the time to think through choices. Is it better to feel badly than share with your friends? Is not listening to your mom worth it when it makes you feel sad and full of regret?

remembrance

(ree-MEM-brens)

noun

An event or act done to help remember a special person, place, or event.

Every year we like to do something as a family in REMEMBRANCE of our grandmother.

Remembrance is a lovely concept, and it's important to take the time to think fondly about a person, place, or activity you did with your family. While it may be possible at times to honor a special person in an elaborate fashion, there are many simpler ways you can go about remembering someone or something. For example, if you'd like to commemorate a particular time—like when you moved into a new house or one of the children graduated—take some time to look at photographs and discuss your memories with your family. The important lesson to impart to your child is that the remembrance itself, and not the way you do it, matters most.

resilience

(ree-ZILL-yens)

noun

The ability to bounce back quickly from a setback or difficulty.

My RESILIENCE helped me to play baseball again, even though I got hurt during the last game.

Adults don't often have the luxury to take time off and escape from the world after suffering a setback, which means that you sometimes have to be resilient. And as you have responsibilities at home and at work that must be met regardless of what you're facing, there are many instances that also require a child to be resilient. It can be difficult for a child to go back to school after having a negative encounter with another child, or to ride a bike again after falling, but by encouraging her to be resilient and get back into the action, you set her up to successfully handle all the difficulties that life will eventually throw at her.

resourceful

(ree-SORCE-full)

adjective

Able to handle an unexpected situation with whatever materials are available to you.

I'm RESOURCEFUL, so I wasn't concerned when we had to change our Halloween costumes right before the party.

It's frustrating to be put in a situation where plans change and things don't work out the way you expected they would. If you're a careful planner, it's easy to become disappointed and annoyed when the circumstances in which you need to function aren't what you expected. However, as an adult, you also know that being resourceful and making do whenever possible is an incredibly valuable skill. When your child is confronted with such a situation, take the time to show him how he can work in a way other than he had planned. Decide together on an alternative course of action. You'll find that he won't be upset the next time he is confronted with a similar situation.

respect

(ree-SPEKT)

noun

A feeling of admiration held toward an object or another person.

I have a lot of RESPECT for the people who took time to volunteer for the school fundraiser.

Because your kids don't always listen or do as they're told, you may feel that they don't respect you. To earn your children's respect you have to show them what it means to be respectful. By being a respectful person toward your friends, your partner, and even your possessions, you demonstrate that respect is a quality that you value and wish to cultivate in your home. Let your children know when their behavior is disrespectful. Tell them about people you respect, why you feel that way, and how you show your admiration.

responsibility

(ree-spon-suh-BILL-ih-tee)

noun

Accountability to someone or something; the authority to make a decision without the aid of others.

Walking my younger brother home from school is a big RESPONSIBILITY.

Adults have an overwhelming amount of responsibility. It's easy to feel pressured by everything you have to do and everyone you have to answer to. A responsible child is well poised to help take care of himself, help with household chores, and even help raise a sibling. But how do you begin to instill a sense of responsibility in a child? Start by giving your child a small task that she is responsible for on a daily basis. Ask her to make her bed, clear the table, or walk the dog. Praise her for a job well done, and slowly begin to add on responsibilities that you know she can handle.

rest

(rehst)

noun

A refreshing break after a period of action or exertion.

We all needed some REST after the long day at the museum.

It often seems that "rest" is a concept that's impossible for children to understand. Their energy levels never seem to wane, and they rarely sit still for more than a few moments. However, it is important for kids to understand that both children and parents benefit from rest. Encourage your child to play on his own, even if only for a few minutes while you relax quietly. Explain to him that by resting his body, even for a short period, he'll have even more energy to run and play afterward.

ritual

(RITCH-oo-ul)

noun

An event performed with ceremonial importance due to a crucial place it holds in your life.

I love the RITUAL of shopping for our family Christmas tree the day after Thanksgiving.

While many people enjoy religious rituals on a regular basis, it's also important to recognize rituals within your own family. Children easily become accustomed to meaningful activities that are performed with regularity. Do you have relatives over for Sunday dinner? Play games on Friday night? Maybe you go camping every summer and you toast marshmallows and tell stories. These events play a significant role in a child's development. When you find your family participating in an activity that makes everyone happy, make it a point to regularly incorporate it into your lives.

rumor

(ROO-mur)

noun

Circulated talk that has no reliability.

The RUMOR that we were moving to another city was completely false.

Everyone remembers a wild rumor from their youth, whether it be something unkind about another student or curious information about a teacher or neighbor. It is extremely painful and awkward to be the subject of a vicious rumor, and unfortunately social media, cell phones, and the Internet make the spreading of rumors easier than ever. Let your child know that rumors are best ignored. An unhappy person or someone who simply doesn't care to back up her information with facts often instigates rumors. Talk to your children about what you would like them to do in the event they are involved in a rumor.

sacred

(SAY-krid)

adjective

Dedicated to or in honor of someone or something, often religious in nature.

The artwork that my grandfather brought from Europe is SACRED to us.

Whether your family practices a religion regularly or not, it's likely that you've exposed your child to items you feel are sacred. These items can range from an object pertaining to your religious worship to a valued photograph of a family member, an item from your youth, or even your family dinnertime. It's important for children to understand that some objects or ideas are held in the highest esteem and must be respected accordingly. Talk to your child about what your family holds sacred. Explain that there is no debating or arguing when it comes to something that is sacred; its importance simply must be accepted.

sadness

(SAD-niss)

noun

Grief or unhappiness.

The SADNESS I felt kept me from wanting to play outside with my friends.

Although parents would like to shelter their children from sadness, it's impossible for a child to not feel sorrow over the loss of a pet, a disappointment at school, or a fight with a friend. While it's expected that a child will feel sadness in those circumstances, let your child know that sometimes people simply feel sad for no particular reason. Everyone has moods; people can't always be positive. Explain that you too feel sad sometimes, but that after a short period your mood always changes for the better. By sharing your experiences with sadness you'll be showing your child that emotions are normal and letting him know that it's okay for his emotions to change from time to time.

satisfaction

(sat-iss-FACK-shun)

noun

The joy that stems from successfully fulfilling a want or need.

We felt such SATISFACTION the day we finished building our tree house.

It's not necessary to do something big—like buying a new wardrobe or taking a long vacation—to feel satisfied. True satisfaction stems from knowing that you have what you need every day. It's possible to feel satisfied by taking stock of various simple accomplishments. Children feel proud when they learn to dress themselves, or read a favorite book. Your pride in such accomplishments is an example of how you can easily feel more satisfied. Give yourself credit for managing your family, your job, and your home so successfully. Seeing you feel satisfaction for your jobs will help your children see that there are constant opportunities to experience satisfaction in everyday life. They will soon understand the joy that stems from taking the time to sit back and appreciate everything they have accomplished.

savor

(SAY-vur)

verb

To enjoy something slowly and with great appreciation.

I decided to SAVOR every single bite of my vanilla cupcake.

Children tend to tear through Christmas and birthday presents as fast as possible and it's rare to see a child savor much of anything. Their entire stash of Halloween candy would last five minutes if parents let them at it all at once. Show your child that, by taking the time to slow down and appreciate something, whether it's a slice of birthday cake or the opening of a special present, the pleasure will last even longer. The next time you're enjoying a favorite meal or activity together, be sure to tell your child how much you're savoring every second. By stopping to appreciate her experiences, your child will be on her way to understanding how to get the most out of life.

security

(sih-KYOOR-ih-tee)

noun

Something that makes you feel safe and protected and that brings you comfort.

I sleep better with the SECURITY of my nightlight and my favorite stuffed animal.

All parents want their children to feel safe and secure, but with small children this isn't always the easiest task to accomplish. Children tend to have a few fears—from the dark to shadows to unfamiliar noises. It's important that you do whatever it takes to make your child feel secure. Bedtime stories, special blankets and toys, or a nightlight are simple ways to bring a child comfort. Let your child know that it's okay to have fears, and that you will be there for him to make sure he is safe.

sensitive

(SEN-sih-tiv)

adjective

Capable of being sympathetic when dealing with the needs or feelings of other people.

I try to be SENSITIVE so that I know when my friends are upset about something.

Adults are able to notice slight changes in a person's demeanor that might suggest she is having trouble, and you've likely been in a situation where you know a friend is having a problem before she actually tells you. Being sensitive to the needs of others is a key component to developing healthy and strong friendships. Talk to your children about how you know when they are upset or need something. Encourage them to be alert for signs that other members of their family or their friends might need some special attention. You'll likely find that your child is more sensitive to others than you ever imagined.

service

(SUR-viss)

noun

Work done by a person out of duty or as a favor.

Since Martin Luther King Day is a national day of SERVICE, I try to do something positive to help my community.

Performing service for your family, congregation, school, or community helps such organizations thrive, and by donating your time, energy, and talent to a cause, you improve the lives of countless other people. Children can benefit greatly from service. While they may be too young to volunteer regularly, talk to them about how they can help their community or school become a better place. Would they enjoy cleaning a park? Helping at a fundraiser? Painting a school? By doing service, your child will be able to enjoy seeing the immediate results of her efforts . . . and will know how much her actions mean to others.

share

(shayre)

verb

To have something in common with another person; the willingness to allow another person to use something of yours.

My next-door neighbor and I SHARE the ability to climb trees very quickly.

All parents have struggled to get their children to share. When another child or a sibling sets his sights on your child's newest toys, don't be surprised to see her suddenly become very possessive. You know that teaching a child to willingly share takes patience and time. It may also be helpful to explain to your child that there is another form of sharing that doesn't involve letting a person play with a toy: She can share traits. Perhaps your child will find it amusing to discover that she shares common interests, food likes and dislikes, and various fears or talents with another friend.

silly

(SILL-ee)

adjective

Not serious or formal.

My entire family likes to act SILLY on Saturday mornings.

It's likely that your children have more on their minds than you did at their age. They are under so much pressure to do well in school, and it's known that children have less time to play overall. In addition, parents are more stressed than ever, with long commutes and even longer work hours. But just being silly with your kids is a great way to bond and burn off stress. Make it a point to forget about your responsibilities from time to time and just play with your kids. Let them decide what it is they want to do . . . whether it's build a pirate ship, have a scavenger hunt, or play hide and seek.

simplicity

(sim-PLISS-ih-tee)

noun

The quality of being uncomplicated or easily grasped.

The theme for the party was brilliant in its SIMPLICITY.

It's easy for simple ideas to become overly complex and it's rare to enjoy something for its simplicity in today's society. Birthday parties are often over the top and play dates are arranged to the last detail long in advance. By taking the time to step back and simplify your life, you will teach your child a good lesson about what matters most. Try stopping over at a neighbor's house to see if the kids want to play; consider hosting a birthday party focused on cake, games, and ice cream. You'll likely discover that by doing this you're getting to the core of what it really is that your child wants.

sincerity

(sin-SERE-ih-tee)

noun

Genuineness and honesty in the expression of thoughts and feelings.

My teacher is an honest person and I never have to question her SINCERITY when she praises me for a job well done.

Sincerity is a quality that adults cherish. It's comforting to know that our friends and coworkers are sincere in their intentions. As a parent, you want to raise a sincere child, and you also want her to be able to tell when someone is being genuine in his actions. Begin by explaining how hurtful it can be when someone is insincere. By stressing how important it is to have honest people in your life, you'll be encouraging your child to aim for sincerity in all of her actions.

society

(suh-SYE-uh-tee)

noun

A structured community of people who share similar traditions or ideas.

If I'm going to be part of our SOCIETY, I need to behave well and be respectful toward others.

While it's important for children to think for themselves and to feel free expressing their opinions, they also need to know that they live in part of a larger society. Children should understand that certain behaviors—like being respectful toward schoolmates and neighbors—are expected when they are at school, or living in a community. Explain what your child needs to do to be a good neighbor or coworker. Let him know that it's important to make sure the needs of others are being met if your larger society is going to be healthy and functional.

sophistication

(suh-fiss-ti-KAY-shun)

noun

Refinement, worldliness, and wisdom.

The SOPHISTICATION of the game made it more exciting and challenging to play.

While you may worry about your child being too sophisticated too soon, it can be healthy for a young person to have an understanding of what makes something sophisticated. Parents tend to shield their children from adult issues and want to find comfortable, child-friendly activities whenever possible. While this makes sense, allowing your children to read a book that's slightly out of reach or watch a movie that they may not fully understand will encourage them to grow intellectually and will pique their interests in the outside world. Remind yourself that "sophisticated" does not always equal inappropriate.

special

(SPESH-uhl)

adjective

Set apart by unusual or distinct characteristics that distinguish a person or item; very worthy or important.

My ability to sympathize with others when necessary makes me SPECIAL.

Adults like to believe that their children know how special they are. It's easy to think that because you love and care for them, they automatically know that they are the most special people in your life. While your children surely feel your love for them, they may not feel that they are special. Be sure to point out all of the qualities in your child that make her special or unique. She may not know how much you value her artistic side, or her ability to be a good friend or sibling. By telling her that she possess special qualities, you'll encourage her to cultivate everything that makes her different or unique.

splurge

(splerj)

verb

To indulge by buying a rare treat or a luxury item.

I was so grateful that my parents decided to SPLURGE and buy me a new bike!

It's incredibly fun to shower a child with special gifts. In fact, one of the best parts of being a parent is seeing the joy on a child's face when he receives a new bike or a special toy, or is told that he's going somewhere he loves. While splurging on a special outing or item is fine, be sure to explain to your child why you've decided to splurge on something. Maybe he did something to deserve it—like improve his grades or consistently do a good job with his chores. Perhaps you received a promotion at work and are feeling especially generous. When your child understands that a special item is a splurge, he'll understand that it is not something that he should expect every day, but that it is something to appreciate and be thankful for.

spontaneity

(spahn-tuh-NAY-ih-tee)

noun

The quick decision to do something without any prior planning.

My uncle's SPONTANEITY always brings fun and surprises.

With all of the planning you do to make life run smoothly, it may seem impossible to do anything spontaneously. But deciding to deviate from your routine and do something unexpected with your kids can be a wonderful way to boost everyone's spirits. By occasionally replacing your Saturday morning errands with an unexpected trip to the beach, you'll show your children that there's more to life than structure and routine. They'll see that life can also be exciting and fun—and they'll look forward to the next time they receive the gift of an unexpected trip.

stability

(stuh-BILL-ih-tee)

noun

The quality of remaining strong and solid regardless of outside circumstances.

My mom works hard to keep us happy and healthy—and to give us all a sense of STABILITY at home.

Parents work hard to maintain a feeling of stability in the lives of their children. You provide a welcoming home, work hard to make sure your family is financially secure, and follow a healthy schedule. That said, you likely know that children get bored easily and tend to thrive on excitement, which can make it difficult to maintain a certain level of stability in their lives. In fact, they may object to simple things like bath time, bedtime, homework sessions, or family meals. Let them know that you have set up this schedule because stability is key to health and happiness, and you'll all feel better as a result.

story

(STORE-ee)

noun

An account of an event that took place, either factual or fictional.

My favorite STORY that my mom tells is about the day I was born.

Your children are undoubtedly familiar with stories; perhaps you read to them nightly or let them enjoy an occasional TV show or movie. But don't forget to explain that stories are part of real life, too. Children and adults learn and remember events more easily when those events are relayed in the form of a story. Encourage storytelling at home . . . talk to your children about your key life events, how they took place, what they were like, how you felt. Also encourage your child to tell you the story of her day. Take interest in what she did, who she played with, and what she learned. Storytelling is a terrific way to develop imagination and grow closer as a family.

strength

(strengkth)

noun

The ability to handle stress, pressure, or other difficult situations.

My STRENGTH kept me from crumbling under the pressure of changing to a new school.

Strength is a word that children often associate with physical ability; however, it is also important for children to know that strength is a remarkable inner quality—and that possessing strength will help them tremendously throughout their lives. Pay attention to situations in which your child demonstrates strength on any level. This could mean forfeiting his turn on the slide at the playground to another child or not getting angry when someone does not want to share. Let your child know that you admire his strength of character.

struggle

(STRUHG-ul)

verb

To put a great amount of effort toward a problem or difficulty.

I had to STRUGGLE to get an A in my science class, but it was completely worth the effort.

You don't want to watch your child struggle emotionally or physically, but you also know that if you were to jump in and help each time your child was struggling, she wouldn't learn how to navigate any difficulties on her own. Make a point of raising a self-sufficient child. Talk to her about any struggles you've faced, how you handled them, and what the ultimate reward was. Your child will soon understand that struggle often brings rewards.

style

(stile)

noun

A unique way of doing something; how you choose to present yourself to the world.

I admire my aunt for her utterly unique sense of STYLE.

Too much concern with brands, clothing, and how a person looks isn't healthy and you don't want your child to be too focused on his appearance. However, encouraging your child to express his own sense of style can be beneficial. While it's nice to think that looks don't matter, how a person presents himself to the world *is* important. Teach your child that style is about presence, poise, and confidence. Encourage him to make unique choices that reflect his own personality.

success

(suk-SESS)

noun

The accomplishment of something you set out to do, whether it be finishing a project you planned or becoming well-known for a particular reason.

My SUCCESS on the high-school soccer team was due to my commitment to daily practice.

When you think about success, it's not unusual to imagine wealth, fame, and notoriety. While that is obviously one way to define success, it's important for your child to understand that little accomplishments can be equally as meaningful. The pride you feel when your child walks for the first time or brings home an excellent report card are examples of you acknowledging her successes. Let your child know that success comes in various sizes, and that she should be proud of every single achievement.

support

(suh-PORT)

verb

To provide strength and guidance to another person during a time of need.

My mom wanted to SUPPORT our neighbors by helping out when they had a new baby.

While you can depend on friends and families in times of crisis, it's not unusual for families to need just a little extra support from time to time. Work and day care schedules often mean that we need to ask for help, such as asking a neighbor for a ride or to sit with your child for a short period. Support is something that all parents need but are often afraid to ask for. Explain to your children that support, even in small doses, can make a world of difference in someone's life. Encourage your child to lighten a neighbor's load by offering to walk her dog, cut her grass, or just help take out the garbage.

surrender

(suh-REHN-der)

verb

To give up control of something due to circumstances beyond your control.

I had to SURRENDER to the fact that the advanced placement science class was just too hard for me.

It is a parent's inclination to teach his or her children to never to give up no matter what, and it's easy to believe that if you simply exert enough effort, any obstacle will eventually be surpassed. However, this approach, while often correct, puts a tremendous amount of pressure on a young person. Adults know what their limitations are—kids don't. Teach your child the difference between giving up without a battle and making a clear decision to surrender. Kids can't succeed at everything they try, and it's healthy for them to understand this.

sympathy

(SIHM-puh-thee)

noun

The expression of sorrow when someone is hurting, or the ability to understand what another person is feeling.

I was able to have SYMPATHY for my friend when he lost his new baseball glove.

The ability to feel sympathy is key to having solid friendships. Adults have had many experiences that enable them to relate to a friend or family member who is experiencing difficulties, but how do you help a child relate to the challenges that her peers face? Sympathy begins by simply showing your child that everyone gets scared, nervous, and anxious at times. The next time your child's friend falls on the playground or misses his mother while at a play date, remind your child that she has been in the same position. This will make it easier for her to comfort a friend who is hurting.

talent

(TAL-ent)

noun

A special natural ability.

It took years for me to discover my TALENT for baking.

Children participate in so many activities from an early age, from ballet and music to baseball and swimming. Perhaps you hope that your child will excel at one or more of these activities, developing a lifelong connection to whatever area she shows talent in. While it's wonderful to have a child who has the potential to be a concert pianist, be sure to celebrate your child's other talents. Perhaps your child is especially adept at making other kids comfortable—or maybe she can draw, can cook, or has a way with animals. All talents should be cherished, even if your child's talent doesn't fall in the area that you hoped it would.

tenacity

(teh-NASS-uh-tee)

noun

The quality of holding firmly to an idea or point of view.

My mother's TENACITY when it came to educational issues inspired everyone.

Adults know how hard a person has to work to get ahead. This can mean moving forward in the workplace, fighting for an important cause in the community, or just sticking to a certain set of ideals. Children can be tenacious in their everyday actions. They have strong beliefs about what is right and wrong, even if this is limited to what they want for lunch or to wear to school. Show them how being tenacious can be an asset. Being tenacious can help your child make it through a hard time and can help him achieve a goal, such as continuing to study something even though he is hitting obstacles, or trying out for a team even though he was cut the previous year. Tell your child about how your tenacity resulted in a positive change in your life.

thrill

(thrill)

noun

An intensely exciting experience.

The THRILL of the experience made me want to go back to the amusement park right away.

It may take the excitement of getting a new car, receiving a major promotion, or taking a faraway trip for you to feel truly thrilled, but fortunately, children can feel thrilled simply by experiencing something new and different. What activities would thrill your child that you haven't gotten around to doing? Maybe your child would love a boat ride or a day trip to a vibrant city that he's never been to. It's easy to get distracted by the responsibilities of everyday life and forget that there are thrilling experiences for your child around every corner. So take the time to do something new—you'll thrive on your child's excitement and be energized by the experience.

treasure

(TREHZH-ur)

noun

Someone or something that is loved and regarded as highly valued.

It makes me feel good that my mom and dad consider the artwork I bring home from school to be a real TREASURE.

When children think of treasure they inevitably imagine a buried trunk overflowing with gold and jewels. But if you think about it, is there a better metaphor for treasure? Take the time to tell your children how you treasure their place in your life. It's also okay to let them know that you treasure objects, too, such as your grandmother's pearls or a piece of artwork you worked long and hard to buy. Encourage your child to treasure good moments, such as family outings and holidays. Also let him know that he is allowed to create a special treasure all of his own, whether it's made up of toys, games, or stuffed animals.

trend

(trehnd)

noun

A fashion or popular concept that is usually temporary.

The TREND at school is to wear purple socks with your Converse.

Trends tend to be incredibly important to kids, and it's natural for them to want what everyone else has, regardless of its practicality or cost. While fashion trends can be frustrating for parents, try to remember that there was a time when you felt that your life depended on getting a certain pair of shoes or jeans. Ideally, you'll have a self-assured child who doesn't feel that her self-worth is defined by a label. However, keep in mind that even the most confident child isn't immune to trends. Decide together which trends are appropriate for your child and which are best ignored.

truth

(trooth)

noun

A fact or statement that conveys what has actually happened.

I didn't want to tell the TRUTH about how I broke the vase, but in the end I decided it was best that I did.

Truth can be a difficult concept for young children. While parents encourage them to tell the truth whenever possible, their imaginations can sometimes make this challenging, and it's natural for a child to sometimes blame spilled juice on a sibling or a pet. Children tend to know when they've done something wrong, but aren't aware of how insignificant most of their mistake are. Explain to your child that everyone makes mistakes. Everyone loses things, breaks things, and spills things. By encouraging your children to always tell the truth about what happened, you put them in a position to always get any help that they need.

unique

(yoo-NEEK)

adjective

Totally different in a very special way or manner.

The artwork my mom makes is completely UNIQUE.

While you may have an appreciation for unique objects, people, or traits, it's not unusual for children to prefer items and concepts that are familiar. Children feel more comfortable when they fit in with their peers, so they may be reluctant to embrace something with unique qualities, even if they find themselves drawn to it. Express your appreciation for unique items whenever you can. Let your child see that you value items for their differences, and she will soon understand that common items aren't as exciting as they might initially seem.

vitality

(vye-TAL-uh-tee)

noun

A joyous and energetic approach to situations and activities.

The VITALITY my little sister brings to everything she does makes her fun to be around.

Children have endless supplies of energy and enthusiasm, and often get to experience situations that evoke unbridled joy. Encourage them to notice the vitality they bring to everyday situations. Let your children know that you appreciate how they become excited by a simple trip to the park or the beach and be sure to tell them that the happiness they inspire in you, as well as in others, will add a fresh energy to their lives.

vocation

(voe-KAY-shun)

noun

A strong feeling that you are destined to follow a particular line of work.

From a very early age, my father knew his VOCATION would be in the arts.

Loving your area of work makes life much easier, and it's a true blessing to feel that you are putting your efforts toward a field that you were meant to work in. Talk to your children about how you came to find your vocation, whether it happens to be what you do for a living or something you do on the side. Explain what's important about your work, how you got there, and what you do to remain engaged and effective at it. Your child may develop interests and talents that will lead him to a particular vocation. Encourage him, and help him develop skills that will help him excel in that area.

volunteer

(voll-uhn-TEER)

verb

To offer your services to a person or organization without the expectation of being paid.

Because I love dogs, I VOLUNTEER at the animal shelter as much as I possibly can.

Between work, kids, chores, shopping, and everything else you do, the idea of incorporating volunteer work into your schedule sounds impossible. If it doesn't seem reasonable to commit your time to a cause on a regular basis, think about what kind of work you can do as a family. Perhaps you can make it an annual event to volunteer at a soup kitchen during the holidays, or maybe your local community needs help cleaning up a park at a certain time each year. By showing your child that service is important, you teach her that she personally has the power to help people and make her immediate world a better place.

wealth

(wellth)

noun

A great abundance of something.

My dad has a WEALTH of knowledge about history and literature.

Money might first come to mind when you think of the word "wealth," but while it's fine for children to understand that wealth can and does refer to money, make sure that they are familiar with other forms of wealth. People may possess a wealth of knowledge, or have lots of friends, a loving family and home, or maybe they have extraordinary talents. Teach your children that having money without family, friends, and joy isn't actually much to rejoice about, but having a wealth of what truly makes them happy is what counts the most.

welcome

(WELL-kuhm)

adjective

Warmly accepted, as into a new home or society.

We wanted our new neighbors to feel WELCOME so we brought them a cake.

It's incredibly difficult being the new person—whether you've changed schools, moved to a new neighborhood, or started a new job—and nothing helps more than being welcomed by other people. Talk to your child about making people feel welcome . . . whether by being kind to a new child at school or making friends feel comfortable when they come over to play. Explain that using manners, being courteous, and finding out what the other person needs are how to make a person feel welcome. Your child will soon instinctively know how to give people what they need, and will carry this trait into adulthood.

well-being

(well-BEE-ing)

noun

A healthy, positive state.

Sleep, good nutrition, exercise, and playing with friends are essential to my WELL-BEING.

While adults know what it takes to maintain a sense of well-being—sleep, healthy foods, fresh air, exercise, good friends, and satisfying work—your children aren't likely to be aware of what keeps them going. Children also are easily upset when they are off their schedules. While they may not be excited to eat their vegetables, brush their teeth, and go to bed on time, explain that all of these activities are essential to a positive sense of well-being. Let them know that you don't feel well when you're off your schedule, and that it's best for them to take care of themselves so they can play, go to school, and enjoy their favorite activities.

wish

(wish)

verb

To express a desire for something to happen or come true.

I WISH that my grandparents didn't live so far away.

Children tend to associate wishes with something like blowing out the candles on a birthday cake—they know how to visualize what they want, but don't necessarily expect it to appear. Many wishes are completely childlike in nature—wishing one could fly, be invisible, or have superhuman powers; however, it's important to let your child know that it's okay to have wishes that she actually wants to come true. It's okay for your child to wish that she could spend more time with friends, take a trip, or get a certain toy, so talk to your kids about what they can do to actually make a wish come true.

wonder

(WUN-der)

noun

A feeling of awe inspired by something very beautiful.

The rainbow was so vibrant that we all stared at it in WONDER.

With so many new experiences to be had, children are fortunate because wonder can be a frequent occurrence for them. This is one area where you have much to gain from your child. A blooming flower, a star in the sky, or even a caterpillar crawling across the sidewalk can invoke a sense of wonder in a child. Take the time to share in their discoveries. Allow yourself to appreciate how inspiring the first flowers of spring are—or how enjoyable it is to experience a starry night. By encouraging your child to cultivate his sense of wonder—and by sharing in his joy—you'll create an appreciation for all of the little things in life.

work

(wurk)

noun

The physical and mental energy required to make or accomplish something.

Gardening on weekends is the most enjoyable WORK I do.

When you're an adult, work tends to mean the efforts you put toward your occupation or raising your children. And while work may simply refer to school activities, homework, and chores for your kids, these actions sow the seeds for a lifetime of appreciating the value of work. Children generally don't want to spend their time making the bed, folding the laundry, and completing math assignments, but by showing them that by helping you they make the household run more smoothly and by completing their schoolwork they are doing what they need to do to get ahead, you'll be well on your way to raising a child with an excellent work ethic.

worry

To experience feelings of anxiety due to something that concerns or scares you.

Sometimes I WORRY about my parents when they are out late at night.

All children worry and, even though you try to make them feel as secure as possible, children naturally develop anxieties. Your child may be afraid of the dark, be upset about trouble at school, or even worry about traveling far from home. While it's impossible to erase every worry from your child's mind, you can comfort him by letting him know that he isn't alone. And, while you may not want to bother a child with typical adult worries, you can talk to him about the fears you had when you were a child. Your child will feel better knowing that Dad was also afraid of the dark and that Mom was scared on the first day of school. Knowing that you are now strong, well-adjusted people will help your child see that his worries will eventually vanish.

worth

(wurth)

noun

The value or goodness of a person or object.

Because I have a strong sense of my own WORTH, I strive to maintain a healthy lifestyle.

Life is so complicated that it's easy to feel frustrated and think that no matter what you do it's never enough, but having a strong sense of self-worth will help you get through difficult times. Talk to your children about valuing their own good qualities. Make sure they have a clear understanding of what makes them special people. Explain that knowing their worth—and what they have to offer the world—will bring confidence, faith, and strength. A sense of their own worth will help them when they are feeling especially low or challenged by life.

Index

About the Author

Paula Balzer is a former literary agent and the author of *Writing & Selling Your Memoir*. Paula's writing has also been seen in *New York Family* magazine where she writes about parenting issues, *Modern Bride* magazine, *Writer's Digest* magazine, and *www.achildgrows.com*, Brooklyn's largest and most popular parenting blog. Paula lives in South Orange, NJ, with her husband and daughters.